D1646921

改编　顾希佳
英文主译　门顺德
翻译组成员　门顺德　王秀杰　李晓霞
孟繁滨　侯奕松　高君　曹盈
英文审校　汪榕培

中国经典文化故事系列

Chinese Classic Cultural Stories Series

中国传统节日趣谈

Traditional Chinese Festivals

廣東省出版集團
全国优秀出版社 广东教育出版社
·广州·

图书在版编目(CIP)数据

中国传统节日趣谈＝Traditional Chinese Festivals：汉英对照／顾希佳改编；门顺德英文主译．—广州：广东教育出版社，2007.9（2008.12重印）
（中国经典文化故事系列）
ISBN 978-7-5406-6754-2

Ⅰ.中…　Ⅱ.①顾…②门…　Ⅲ.①英语—汉语—对照读物②节日—风俗习惯—中国　Ⅳ.H319.4: K

中国版本图书馆CIP数据核字（2007）第134939号

广东教育出版社出版发行
（广州市环市东路472号12-15楼）
邮政编码：510075
网址：http://www.gjs.cn
广东新华发行集团股份有限公司经销
佛山市浩文彩色印刷有限公司印刷
（南海区狮山科技工业园A区）
850毫米×1168毫米　32开本　6.75印张　200 000字
2007年9月第1版　2008年12月第2次印刷
印数：3001－4000册
ISBN 978-7-5406-6754-2
定价：12.10元
质量监督电话：020-87613102　购书咨询电话：020-34120440

CONTENTS 目录

一、春节

1. The Spring Festival

春节，俗称“新年”，是中华民族历来最隆重的节日。

The Spring Festival, also called “the Chinese New Year”, has been the most significant and celebrated holiday of the year for the Chinese nationality.

我们往上追溯，至少在殷墟出土的甲骨文中，就已经出现“年”这个字了。那是刻成一个人弯着背肩负沉甸甸穗禾形状的象形字。可见早在殷商时代，就把“年”和作物收成联系在了一起。《穀梁传·宣公十六年》:“五谷皆熟为有年。五谷大熟为大有年。”《说文解字》释“年”字，也说:“谷熟也。”如今人们常说“年成”、“年景”，也是这个意思。农业社会里，庄稼一年熟一次，庄稼熟了，年也到了，很好记。

The Chinese character *nian* (year) can be traced back to inscriptions on tortoise shells unearthed in the Yin Remains. The pictograph *nian* was carved in the shape of a man bent with heavy ears of wheat on his back, which was an indication that *nian* has been closely related to the harvest ever since the Yinshang Period (1600 BC — 1046 BC). It was recorded in the *Guliang Commentary, the 16th Year of Duke Xuan* that

"New Year is the time of harvest, and a good year is a bumper crop." "Year" is interpreted as "crops are ripe" in *Shuowen Jiezi* (*Explanation and Stady of Principles of Composition of Characters*) written in the Han Dynasty (206 BC—220 AD), which is similar in meaning to "harvest of the year" nowadays. Since the crops are ripe once a year in agricultural societies, New Year approaches at the harvest time.

究竟把哪一天定为"年"，这就要涉及历法。历史上有过不同的历法，定出来的日子也不一样。汉武帝时，创制"太初历"，确立以夏历正月初一为岁首。《史记》、《汉书》称正月初一为"四始"，也就是岁之始、时之始、日之始、月之始；"三朝"，也就是岁之朝、月之朝、日之朝。从此以后，把夏历正月初一叫做"元旦"，沿用了两千多年。这就是说，历史上一般把过年的日子叫"元旦"。以前也有"春节"，一般是指"立春"这一天，和今天所说的春节不是一回事。

Which date is set as the beginning of the Chinese New Year? This has to do with the Chinese calendar. The date of the Chinese New Year varied throughout history due to different Chinese calendars. During the period of Emperor Wu in the Han Dynasty (206 BC — 220 AD), the Taichu Calendar was created, and the beginning of a new year was set on the first day of the first lunar month in the traditional Chinese calendar. The first day of the first lunar month is regarded as "four beginnings" in both *Shiji* (*Records of the Historian*) and *Hanshu* (*Chronicles of the Han Dynasty*), that is, the beginning of a year, the beginning of a time, the beginning of a day, and the beginning of a month. It is also called "three dawns" — the dawn of a year, the dawn of a month, and the dawn of a day. The first day of the first lunar month was kept as "the Chinese New Year" in the following 2,000 years. The day on which people celebrate New Year was usually called *Yuandan* (the Chinese New Year) in history. The Spring Festival used to refer to the Beginning of Spring, which is different from what it means now.

辛亥革命以后，废除夏历，中国开始用公历，就把公历1月1日叫做元旦，称夏历正月初一为春节。从此以后，中国人便有了每年要过两个年的风俗。不过在民众中间，还是约定俗成，只把过春节当做真正意义上的过年，并且总是把年过得红红火火、热热闹闹的。

After the Revolution of 1911, the traditional Chinese calendar was abolished, and the Gregorian calendar was adopted. January 1st is called *Yuandan* (New Year), while the first day of the first lunar month is named the Spring Festival. Therefore, the Chinese people have got the custom of celebrating two New Years. The populace at large tend to celebrate the Spring Festival as the real New Year with

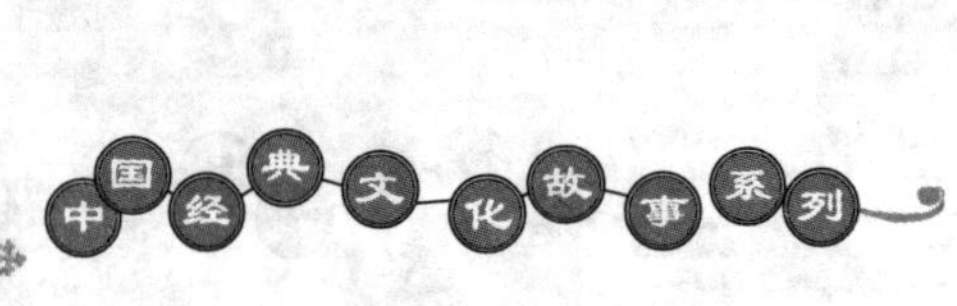

continuous festive celebrations.

春节的风俗，古代有祭祀、朝会、宴饮、占卜、迎神、贺年、玩赏等等内容，随着岁月流逝，这些内容也在发生变迁；各民族、各地域的做法又不尽相同，我们无法一一细说。这里只能大致上作些介绍。

In ancient times, the celebrations of the Spring Festival included offering sacrifices to ancestors, making an audience with the emperor in the morning, holding feasts, telling fortune, welcoming the God, paying a New Year call, and attending entertainments, etc. The customs varied with the passage of time, differed between regions and ethnic groups, and cannot be covered in every detail. The following is only a brief introduction to the custom.

旧时过年，一般都在上一年的十二月二十三日就拉开序幕了。一般要扫尘，也就是打扫卫生，还要置办年货、裁制新衣、祭灶、祀祖等，十分忙碌。

The 23rd day of the twelfth lunar month was the prologue to the Spring Festival celebrations in the past. There would be a tight schedule of thorough cleanings, special purchases for the Spring Festival, tailoring of new clothes, worshipping the Kitchen God, and offering sacrifices to the ancestors.

从前，家家户户都在灶间供奉“灶君司命”，俗称“灶王爷”。传说他是被玉皇大帝派到每户人家来保护和监察这一家人的神灵。旧时的灶头上有个灶王龛，贴一张神像。神像上画一个灶王爷，也有的画一男一女，或一男二女，女的就是灶王奶奶。灶王神像两旁贴一副对联：“上天言好事，下界保平安”，正好说明了这个神灵的职责。据说灶王爷平时留在家中，到了每年的腊月二十三日或是二十四日，就要上天去汇报这户人家这一年的品行。这件事关系到家家户户的命运，所以不能马虎，要像模像样地送一送。送灶神上天的仪式，俗称“送灶”。

Every household used to make offerings to *Zaojun* or the Kitchen God, who was said to be appointed by the Jade Emperor of Heaven to protect and monitor each household. A shrine to the Kitchen God was displayed above the kitchen range with a picture of the God on it. On the picture was drawn the Kitchen God, or sometimes a male and a female, or a male and two females. The female was the Kitchen Goddess. Poetic couplets were written on both sides of the picture, on which his duty was expressed as "To Report Good Deeds in Heaven, To Bless People on Earth". It was said that the Kitchen God stayed at people's homes during the year except that he would go to Heaven on the 23rd or 24th day of the 12th month of the lunar year to report the family's behavior to the Jade Emperor. Since the report would determine the destiny of each household, people would hold a kitchen memorial ceremony, or a send-off ceremony as it was commonly called.

送灶在黄昏时举行，要用香烛、供品祀奉，供品中必定有饴糖，据说这是为了让他甜甜嘴，有的说是要让饴糖粘住他的牙，让他无法说坏话。也有的地方让灶君吃酒糟，也是为了使他醉醺醺的，就不再说坏话了。看起来，这是人们在耍弄小聪明，为的是保护自己。最后将神像揭下焚烧，意味着灶君"升天"。有的地方，这时候还有一些人会挨家上门唱歌跳舞，同时向主人乞讨，称为"送灶神"。

The ceremony was held at dusk, with incense, candles and offerings. Maltose was a must to make the God honey-mouthed or to stick his teeth together so that he would not speak ill. In some regions, people would offer him distillers' grains to make him drunk so that he would not speak ill. People played these tricks to protect themselves. After the offerings, the picture was torn off and burned to send the Kitchen God to Heaven. Then people in some regions would go from door to door, singing, dancing and asking for a treat, which was the send-off ceremony of the Kitchen God.

到了除夕夜，还要“接灶”。意思是要把灶神再从天上接回来，也有一个祭祀仪式，把新的一张灶君神像贴到灶王龛里。

On the Chinese lunar New Year's Eve, people will hold a welcome ceremony — to paste a new picture of the Kitchen God above the kitchen range to welcome him back from Heaven.

“爆竹一声除旧，桃符万象更新。”这副尽人皆知的春联正好勾勒出春节风俗中最引人注目的两个事象：放爆竹、贴春联。

"Firecrackers Ring out the Old, Couplets Ring in the New", the well-known couplets sketch the two highlights of the Spring Festival: setting off firecrackers and pasting Spring Festival couplets.

爆竹的初意是辟疫驱厉。南朝梁的时候就有这种风俗了。古人以为山里有一种精怪，名叫山魈，常来捣乱。人们把竹子捆成一捆，放在火里烧，发出噼里啪啦的声响，山魈害怕了，就逃走了。后来，这种爆竹逐渐演变，成为鞭炮，后来又有了烟火。当然，放爆竹，它的原始意义早已淡化，如今只是图个喜庆热闹而已。

The original meaning of setting off firecrackers was to exorcise the devils and diseases as well. This custom dates back to the Liang Period (502 AD—557 AD) of the Southern Dynasties (420 AD — 589 AD). A demon in the mountains named Mandrill always made trouble. The crackings of the burning bamboos tied together would frighten the Mandrills away. Later on, the burning bamboos evolved into firecrackers and then fireworks. The setting off of firecrackers has lost its original intent, and is now a way of celebration.

春联，起源于古代的"桃符"。古人在桃木片上写神荼、郁垒二神的名字，春节时挂在门口，以为就可以使恶鬼望而生畏，不敢进门骚扰了。这是在那个时代里人们的一种想法。五代以后，开始在桃板上书写联语。到了明代，又把桃木板改成纸，就和今天的春联很相似了。许多地方的风俗，不仅大门上要贴春联，屋里屋外凡是可以张贴的地方，新年里也都要张贴一些字画。年画的起源，也与桃符有关。先是把门神绘在桃符上，久而久之，绘画的题材趋向世俗化。还有的要倒贴一个"福"字，或是剪各种窗花来粘贴，或是悬挂中国结，说到底，都是为了趋吉避凶。民国初年，有人把年画和月历结合起来，以后就逐渐演变成为挂历，风靡全国。

The Spring Festival couplets originated from peachwood charms in ancient times. On the peachwood charms were written the names of the two Gods "Shentu" and "Yulei". At the time of the Spring Festival, the peachwood charms were hung up at the doorway. Once it was generally accepted that devils would be terrified by the sight of peachwood charms so that they would be kept away from the house and from bothering people. People began to write couplets first on peachwood after the Five Dynasties (907 AD—960 AD), and then on paper until the Ming Dynasty (1368 AD—1644 AD), which bore a striking similarity to the modern practice. Quite a few regions observe the Spring Festival by pasting couplets not only at doorway, but also inside and outside of the houses. Some calligraphies and paintings are put up on the wall as well. The New Year paintings also originated from peachwood charms. The theme of the paintings was merely about the Door God. It later developed into various subjects of social conventions. The Chinese character "Fu" (meaning "blessing" or "happiness") is usually pasted upside down (in Chinese the "reversed Fu" is homophonic with "Fu comes"). Windows are decorated with paper-cuts and the Chinese knots are hung to pursue fortune and avoid disasters. In the early years of the Republic of China (1912 AD — 1949 AD), the New Year paintings were combined with the monthly calendars, which later developed into wall calendars and became popularized throughout the country.

大年三十又称除夕，一般要在家中祭祖。全家人团聚，吃年夜饭。年夜饭总是特别丰盛，让全家人都吃个痛快。古时，人们要喝屠苏酒，据说这是名医华佗发明，后来又由名医孙思邈流传开来的。北方人过年还喜欢吃饺子，饺子像元宝，象征着新年大发财。有人说，这是另一个名医张仲景发明的，他看到寒冬把穷人的耳朵都冻烂了，便配制一种“祛寒娇耳汤”，送给穷人治冻伤。这种很像耳朵的药膳，后来就演变成了饺子。当然，很多风俗的形成往往有个漫长的过程，和我们在这儿说的一些传说掌故并没有真正的关系。不过千百年来人们一直这么口耳相传着，这里寄托着人们对历史的理解和对生活的感情，还是很值得我们去体味的。

The 30th of the twelfth lunar month is also known as the Chinese New Year's Eve, on which people would always stay indoors to offer sacrifices to ancestors. All the family members get together to have the family reunion dinner, which is always luxurious. In ancient times, people would drink “Tusu spirits”, which was said to be invented by the famous doctor Hua Tuo and popularized by another famous doctor Sun Simiao. People in northern China eat *jiaozi*, which takes the shape of gold ingot from ancient China. People eat them and wish for money and treasure in the coming new year. According to one legend, *jiaozi* was invented by another famous doctor Zhang Zhongjing. At the sight of the frostbite on his patients' ears, he compounded decoctions of Chinese medicinal herbs to dispel cold and soften the skin of the ear. The medicinal cuisine looked like ears and later developed into *jiaozi*. Obviously, the development of customs usually undergoes a slow process, and may not necessarily be associated with the above-mentioned legends. Over the years, these legends have been passed down orally. People's understanding of history and their deep affection for life are implied in the legends and are worth our appreciation.

除夕要守岁，从吃年夜饭开始，一家人在一起边吃边聊天，一直要到深夜，迎接新年的到来。在许多地方，除夕夜灶膛里的火是不可以熄灭的，人们会在灶膛里，或是瓦盆里煨上一段粗壮的树根，或是炭结，让它一直燃到年初一，象征着薪尽火传，绵绵不绝。这里似乎有着对远古时代“火崇拜”的依稀回忆，很是耐人寻味。

According to the custom, people will stay up late on the Chinese New Year's Eve. Family members have dinner together, and chat till midnight to welcome the New Year in. In most areas, the fire in the chamber of the kitchen range should not be put out on the eve. People will place a thick tree root or a carbon block in the range or in an earthen basin, to let it burn until the first day of the lunar New Year. As one piece of fuel is consumed, the flame passes to another. It symbolizes eternity, and has a hint of the worship of fire as in ancient times.

守岁又称“熬年”，这里也有个故事。说是从前有一种凶恶的怪兽，人称“年”。每当除夕夜就会出来伤害人畜。人们为了躲避它，除夕夜早早关门，不敢睡觉，坐等天亮，所以称为“熬年”。到了年初一，大家出来一看，都还活着，于是相互祝贺，表示庆幸，如此而已。据说有一个除夕夜，“年”窜进江南一个村庄，吃掉很多人。有一家挂红布帘，穿红衣服的新婚夫妻安然无恙。还有一家小孩在院子里点燃一堆竹子玩耍，也没事。人们这才明白过来，原来年兽怕红，怕光，怕响声。于是相沿成习，过年的时候要贴红纸，穿红衣，挂红灯，敲锣打鼓，燃放爆竹，据说就是这个缘故。

Staying up on the eve is also called “Survive the *Nian*”, derived from a story. In the good old times, there was a beast called *Nian*, which came out to hurt people and animals on the New Year’s Eve. To keep away from it, people would close doors early and stay awake till daybreak, so it is called “Survive the *Nian*”. On the 1st day of the first lunar month, people would congratulate each other on their survivals. It was said that once on a New Year’s Eve, *Nian* ran into a small village to the south of Yangtze River, and devoured a lot of people. A newly-married couple in red with red door curtains stayed sound and safe. Another family survived because their kids burned a pile of bamboos in the yard. It occurred to people that red, light and loud sound were the things the Beast *Nian* feared most. The customs of pasting red paper-cuts, wearing red dresses, hanging red lights, beating drums and gongs, and setting off firecrackers have been carried on from generation to generation.

除夕夜，习俗又以为是老鼠娶亲的好日子。鼠是十二生肖之一，它的繁殖能力极强。古人渴望多子多孙，给老鼠办婚礼，也就有祈求多子多福的喻义在里面。也有人说，这里还有禳鼠的意思，把老鼠这个祸祟客客气气地“嫁”出去，也是一种驱逐的手段。旧时年画，就有“老鼠娶亲”，画面上一支喜气洋洋的迎亲队伍，清一色的老鼠，个个十分可爱，而在这支队伍的最前面，却偏偏蹲着一只笑容可掬的猫儿。这幅年画的创作意图，很值得咀嚼一番。

Another story of the New Year's Eve says that it is the best wedding date for rats. The rat is one of the Chinese Zodiac Symbols with enormous reproductive capacity. People in ancient times were eager to have more descendants. Holding wedding ceremonies for rats implies their wishes of having more sons and more blessings. Others believe that marrying off the rat is a polite way of exorcizing rat-afflicted disasters.

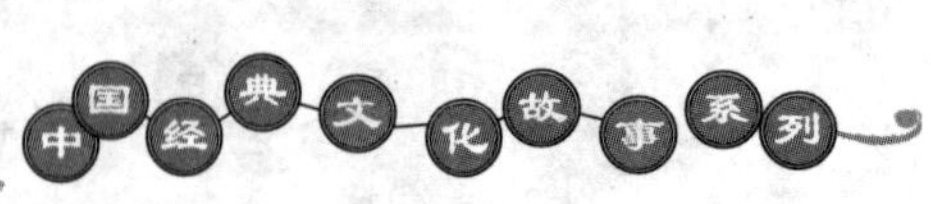

The old-time New Year paintings had a theme of "Rat's Taking a Wife", with a merry wedding parade of lovely rats. The originality of the work lay in the smiley cat squatting in front of the parade.

除夕夜，还有到寺庙里去"宿山守夜"，准备等到子时一过，就到佛前去点燃新年里的第一炷香的这样一种习俗。

Some people spent the New Year's Eve in a vigil in the temples so as to light the first joss stick before Buddha after 1 a.m.

年初一，是新的一年的开始，除了放爆竹之外，就是拜年。一是家里人相互拜年。大家穿上新衣服，按照辈分大小拜年。先拜天地神祇，再拜祖宗，然后是晚辈向长辈行礼，说祝福话，长辈则要给孩子们压岁钱。有的地方有在新年里祭扫祖坟的习惯。有的地方又有在新年里悬挂祖宗肖像，让后代子孙瞻仰祖宗遗容的风俗。二是亲戚朋友之间的相互拜年，请吃年酒，通常会持续到元宵节，才大致告一段落。俗语说，"亲戚是条龙，不来就要穷。"许多人都是把新年里走亲戚当成一件大事来做的。在一些少数民族之间，也盛行拜年。藏族拜年要敬献哈达，回族拜年则互送香油。这里充溢着浓浓的亲情、乡情，令人难以忘怀。

The first day of the first lunar month is the beginning of a Chinese New Year. Besides setting off firecrackers, people would pay New Year visits. Firstly, they extend New Year greetings to family members. All in new clothes, they give their wishes to each other according to different ranks in the family hierarchy. They worship Gods of Earth and Heaven, then ancestors. Juniors salute and extend greetings to seniors. Then children will get money from their seniors as a New Year gift. In some areas, people offer sacrifices at the graves of their ancestors. In other regions, portraits of ancestors are hung to let the descendants look at their ancestors' remains with reverence. Secondly, people pay New Year visits to friends and relatives. The visits and banquets last until the Lantern Festival. As a saying goes, "Relatives are like dragons, and you will become poor without people's visits". People attach great importance to New Year's visits. Some ethnic groups also celebrate the Spring Festival and pay New Year visits. The Tibetans present *hada*, a long piece of silk used as a greeting gift. People of the Hui ethnic group exchange sesame oil. These customs embody people's affection for their hometown and their loved ones.

旧时在汉族士大夫之间，还流行相互投贺名帖的风俗。这是因为亲朋好友太多，登门拜访实在是走不过来，于是想出了这么个简便的办法，派人到处去送名片，称为"飞片"、"飞帖"。有的大户人家干脆准备一本"门簿"，让门房登记客人的往来和"飞片"。在杭州，当年的人们为了表示自家的身份和讨个

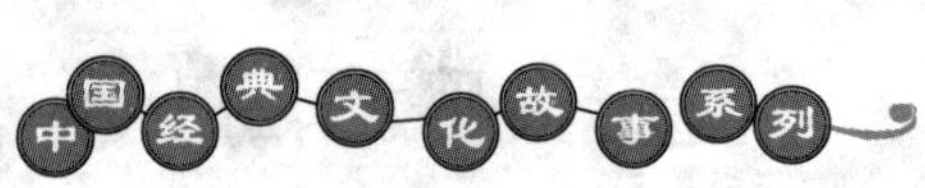

吉利，就总要在门簿的第一页上虚拟四位“亲自上门拜年”的“贵客”：一曰寿百龄老太爷，住百岁坊巷；一曰富有余老爷，住元宝街；一曰贵无极大人，住大学士牌楼；一曰福照邻老爷，住五福楼。爱虚荣和祈福趋利的心态可见一斑。这种投贺名帖的习俗绵延至今，也就是十分流行的贺年片。

One popular convention in the past was to exchange New Year’s name cards among the Han scholar-officials (in feudal China). People could not afford to call on relatives and friends in person, thus inventing the custom of sending name cards everywhere, also called “flying cards” or “flying notes”. A visitor’s book was adopted in large families to keep record of visits and “flying cards” at the gatehouse. To show their social status and seek good luck, people in Hangzhou would imagine four distinguished guests, who visited “personally”, on the first page of their visitor’s book: Lord Centenarian who lived in Alley One-Hundred Age; Lord Excessive-Wealth who lived in Street Gold Ingot; Lord Infinite-Honor who lived in Pailou (monumental gateway) Secretary of the Grand Council (highest rank in feudal China’s imperial official hierarchy); and Lord Luck-to-Neighbors who lived in Tower of Five Lucks. It is evident that people at that time wanted to pray for blessings, seek profit and pursue vanity. The custom has been carried on from generation to generation, and sending New Year’s name cards and New Year’s cards retains its popularity today.

从前，农村还有在新年里看风云、观日色、测晴雨、看参星、听雷鸣、看征兆等一系列占卜年岁丰歉的俗信。滚龙舞狮、扭秧歌、看花灯等娱乐活动更是随处可见。新年是新的一年的开始，除旧迎新，人人都想求个吉利，于是便又有了许多言行上的讲究。说话，要说好话，要图个吉利。比如把橘子、荔枝放在小孩的枕边，为的是求它的谐音“吉利”。如果小孩不小心摔破了碗，要说成是“岁岁平安”。“碎”和“岁”谐音，这一说，就意味着逢凶化吉。新年里一般不扫地，据说扫地是会把运气、财气扫走的。如果一定要扫，也得从外头扫到里边。新年里不打骂孩子，也告诫孩子们不要吵架，相互间说话要留神。亲友们见了面，一开口就是“恭喜发财”，这样一种心态，也是可以理解的。

In the rural areas, in order to predict crop yields, a series of divination customs are observed, including observation of wind, cloud and sunlight, weather forecast, observation of the Three Stars, listening to thunder, and looking for indications. The lively atmosphere also permeates streets and lanes. Entertainment activities such as lion dancing, dragon dancing, *yangge* dancing, and festive lantern watching will be held everywhere. The Chinese are particular about their words and deeds at the beginning of a year. Pleasant words are said for luck. Oranges and litchis are put beside children's pillows, for in Chinese, their pronunciations, respectively "juzi" and "lizhi" mean auspiciousness. If a child breaks a bowl by accident, "Peace all year round" should be said to turn an ill luck into good, as "broken" has the same pronunciation with "year" in Chinese. Sweeping floors is forbidden as it may sweep away luck and fortune. If the floor does need sweeping, people should start from the outside to the inside. An adult should not beat or curse children during the Spring Festival, and children are told to speak gently and not to quarrel with each other. When meeting with relatives and friends, people usually greet each other by saying "Wish you prosperity".

年初三，俗称"小年朝"。旧时有在除夕夜"封井"的习俗，那么到了年初三就要"开井"。人们在井台边祭祀井神，把除夕夜所封的红纸条揭去，表示从这天开始，又可以汲用井水了。

The third day of the New Year is colloquially called "Xiaonianzhao (preliminary year's dawn)". As tradition goes, the well is capped on the New Year's Eve, and uncapped on the third day of the New Year. The red paper on the well is uncovered, and sacrifices are offered at the well head to the Well God. From this day on, water can be drawn from the well.

年初五，烧纸敬神，称为"烧五纸"。古代有"五祀"。后来又有了五路财神。每到年初五，都要祭祀五路财神，商家则尤其重视。

On the fifth day of the New Year, people would burn sacrificial paper, which is known as *Shaowuzhi* (burning paper as sacrificial offerings on the fifth day). In ancient times, there were "five worships", which later developed into the five Gods of Wealth. On this day, the Chinese, businessmen in particular, offer sacrifices to the five Gods of Wealth.

年初七是"人日"。据汉代东方朔《占书》载，岁后八日，一日鸡、二日犬、三日猪、四日羊、五日牛、六日马、七日人、八日谷。习俗以为，如果这一天晴，就预兆所主之物兴旺发达；如果阴，则预兆有灾祸。我们说，自然界某些前兆现象往往蕴涵一些道理，但将它无限扩大，来预测人事，则不足取。不过由此而留下来的一些习俗，就又是一回事了。比如在一些地方，年初七贴个纸人在帐子上，或是屏风上，还要吃七种菜做成的羹，说是为了表示对"人"的尊重。这样一层意思，倒也是蛮好的。

The seventh day of the New Year is "Man's Day". As recorded in *Zhan Shu* (Book on Divination) by Dongfang Shuo of the Han Dynasty (206 BC—220 AD), the first eight days of the lunar New Year are respectively designated as the days of the rooster, dog, pig, sheep, ox, horse, man and grain. Sunny weather is an indication of the flourishing of the things symbolized by these days, while cloudy days stand for disaster. The omens of Nature may imply some principles, but cannot be overstated to predict occurrences in human life. The customs derived from these legends are a different story. Paper-cut men are pasted on tents or screens. A soup made of seven vegetables is served to show respect to people, the implication of which is well-intended.

再过几天，很快就要进入元宵灯会的另一番热闹之中。人们常常以为，过年是要过到元宵才算结束的。有些话，就留在下一节里去说吧。

The Lantern Festival comes a few days later. The celebration of the Spring Festival does not come to an end until this day. More will be covered in the following chapter.

二、元宵节

2. The Lantern Festival

元宵节，又称“上元节”、“元夕节”、“灯节”。正月十五闹元宵，同样由来已久。这是一年当中第一个月圆的夜晚，人们张灯结彩，走上街头，通宵达旦，欢度节日，总是会留下深刻的印象。

The Lantern Festival is also known as the Shangyuan Festival, the Yuanxi Festival or the Yuanxiao Festival. And the celebration of the Lantern Festival on the 15th day of the first lunar month also has a very long history. The 15th day is the first night to see a full moon in a new year and every house is decorated with lanterns and streamers. As night falls, people go in crowds to admire the colorful and impressive lanterns in streets. The celebration leaves deep impressions on anyone who joins it.

元宵节的形成，可能要追溯到古人对火的崇拜。也有人认为它与佛教、道教都有某种联系。古代傩祭，要点燃火把，用来逐疫驱鬼，不过在时间上还并不是定在正月十五。东汉明帝曾经下令，元宵节不论士族庶民一律挂灯，开创了先例。到了隋炀帝的时候，则已形成定制，每年正月十五夜晚，京城里总要“大列炬

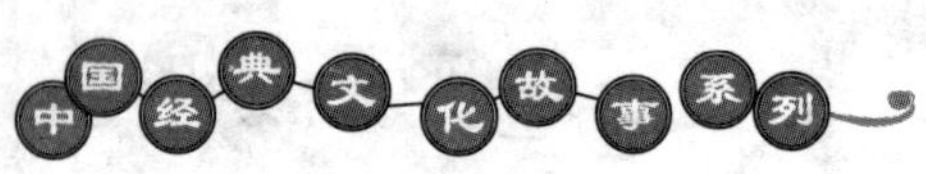

火，光烛照地，百戏之盛，振古无比”，几万人走上街头狂欢，说元宵节这时候已蔚然成风，大概是比较稳妥的。此后，历代帝王又有意倡导，上行下效，愈演愈烈。唐代实行宵禁，夜晚不准出行，唯独在元宵节，皇帝特许开禁三天，称为“放夜”。宋代，又延长到五夜。明代愈发开放，规定正月初八上灯，十七落灯，前后狂欢十夜。《福建通志》里记载了一段轶闻，说是蔡君谟任福州太守时，下令民间每家点灯七盏，等于是一种“硬性摊派”。有人故意做了盏大灯，上面题写一首诗：“富家一盏灯，太仓一粒粟；贫家一盏灯，父子相对哭。风流太守知不知，犹恨笙歌无妙曲！”蔡君谟看到了，当即“还舆罢灯”，看来他是有所触动，认为别人的批评是有道理的。这段轶闻是否有夸饰，已经很难考证了，不过从中折射历史，说明风俗的形成往往与“上行下效”有某种关系，倒是很值得我们重视。元宵节先是在京城里酝酿成熟，后来扩布到各地的城市，然后不断蔓延，直到穷乡僻壤，人们也总是会张罗着过这个节，这样一种流播的轨迹，显而易见。

The Lantern Festival may originate from the fire worship by the ancient people. It is also said to have something to do with Buddhism and Taoism. According to the belief of the ancient people, when they offered sacrifices to their ancestors, fire was lit to alleviate illness and ward off evil spirits. But the day of sacrifices was not exactly on the 15th day of the first lunar month. It was Emperor Ming of the Eastern Han Dynasty (25 AD — 220 AD) who first ordered his people, whether rich or poor, to display lighted lanterns during the

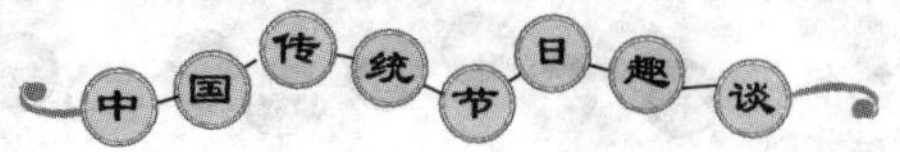

Lantern Festival. This was formalized by Emperor Yang of the Sui Dynasty (581 AD—618 AD). As can be seen from the historical records about the nights of the Lantern Festival every year in the capital city—the magnificent lanterns displayed lit up the night sky and the great scene of performances were unparalleled—the Lantern Festival had developed into a great trend by that time. It was then promoted and enforced by later emperors and became increasingly popular. In the Tang Dynasty (618 AD—907 AD), due to the curfew, people could only go out at night during the three-day Lantern Festival. In the Song Dynasty (960 AD—1279 AD), the festival celebration lasted for five days. However, the grandest celebration took place in the Ming Dynasty (1368 AD—1644 AD), during which the festivities lasted for ten days from the eighth day to the seventeenth day of the first lunar month. A story in *Fujian Annals* says that once Cai Junmo, Prefect of Fuzhou, ordered every household to light seven lanterns on the Lantern Festival, which was beyond the means of common people. So someone deliberately made a big lantern, with a sarcastic poem written on it:

A lantern for a rich family is like a drop in the ocean,
A lantern for a poor family makes the father and the son cry to each other;
Does the merry Prefect know about this?

He is still complaining that the music is not good enough. It seemed that Cai Junmo was touched by the poem and withdrew the order. Though it is difficult to prove what really happened at that time, this significantly mirrors the fact that customs were formed when people followed the examples of their superiors. The activities of the Lantern Festival started from the capital city, and then spread to many of the big cities and later to poor little villages. Obviously this is how customs came into being.

元宵节的内容很丰富，最引人注目的自然是灯彩。灯又有挂灯和迎灯两类。挂灯是家家户户挂灯，或是在街路上扎灯悬灯。人们出来逛街，一边观赏，一边品评，看谁的灯漂亮、华丽、别致。迎灯是人们手里提着灯在街上走，甚至还会形成浩

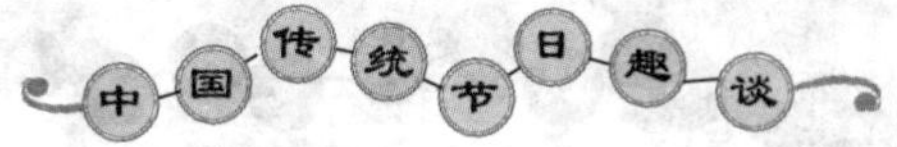

浩荡荡的迎灯队伍。迎灯队伍里往往会有各种各样的民间歌舞表演，热闹非凡。在北方，一般称为闹社火，花样之多，不胜枚举。耍龙灯，舞狮子，划旱船，踩高跷，扭秧歌，以及各种台阁、器乐演奏、戏曲人物扮演、滑稽小丑、武术杂技，可以说是应有尽有。当然，人们又总是会把这一天夜晚的这种活动统称之为迎灯。如果说挂灯是一种造型艺术，那么迎灯就是传统的行为艺术了。

Among various activities during the Lantern Festival, colorful lanterns are the most eye-catching. There are two kinds of lanterns, namely hanging-lanterns and carrying-lanterns. Hanging lanterns decorate households and streets. While strolling around, people appreciate and comment on the magnificence and novelty of the lanterns. Carrying-lanterns are for people to carry along. These people sometimes even join together and merge into a parade, in which folk songs and dances are joyfully performed. In Northern China, such traditional festivities are called *Shehuo*, which involves all kinds of performances, such as the dragon-lantern dance, the lion-dance, the land-boat dance, the *yangge*-dance, walking on stilts, instrumental performances, the characters in Chinese operas shows, clown shows, martial arts and acrobatics. It is true that these activities are also generally referred to as Lantern-carrying, which can be considered as performance arts, compared to Lantern-hanging as plastic arts.

悬挂着供人观赏的灯，逐渐地就形成了展览。各地的能工巧匠在这方面表现出惊人的聪明才智，个个别出心裁，令人叹为观止。北京的宫类、天津的宝莲灯、苏杭的花灯、广州的鸳鸯戏莲灯、东北的冰灯，举不胜举，往往都有鲜明的地方特色和独特的艺术风格。有一种称为“孔明灯”的，很像今天的热气球，利用冷热空气质量不同的原理，居然可以把灯升到空中去。还有一种走马灯，也是利用热空气上升的驱动力，让灯彩自己转动，人们观赏着灯彩各个侧面的绘画造型，格外引人入胜。

Hanging lanterns for viewing has gradually developed into an exhibition. Skillful lantern craftsmen from all over China are admired for their unusual talents and wisdom. The lanterns they make are famous for their local characteristics and unique artistic styles, such as Beijing's Palace Lantern, Tianjin's Lotus Lantern, Suzhou and Hangzhou's Flower Lantern, Guangzhou's Lantern of Mandarin-ducks Playing Joyfully in the Lotus Flowers, and Northeastern China's Ice Lantern. The Kongming Lantern, based on the fact that hot air is lighter than cool air, can even fly like today's hot air balloons. Another lantern called the Running-horse Lantern can revolve by itself because of the heated air in it. At the same time people are fascinated by the shapes of the lanterns and the paintings on them.

在灯彩上写谜语，让别人猜，这就是灯谜。一般认为，南宋

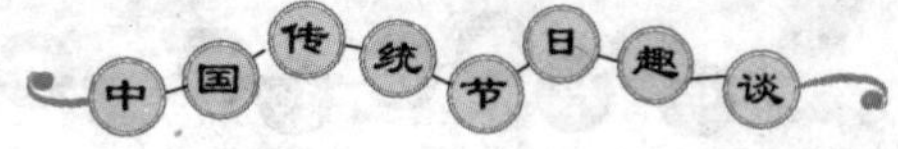

时，京城临安（今杭州）就已盛行灯谜。

Lantern riddles are riddles stuck on the surface of lanterns for people to guess while enjoying the lantern displays. It is generally believed that it was popular in the City of Lin'an (the present-day Hangzhou), the capital of the Southern Song Dynasty (1127 AD — 1279 AD).

关于灯谜，有个蛮风趣的传说。据说当年有个财主，经常欺压穷人。青年王少心里气不过，就在元宵夜扎了盏花灯，上面写了一首诗，有心到财主家去出一口恶气。财主一看花灯，上面写着："头尖身细白如银，论秤没有半毫分，眼睛长到屁股上，光认衣裳不认人。"财主以为是在骂他势利，不觉恼羞成怒，就要家丁去抢花灯。王少却笑嘻嘻地说："你怎么知道我在骂你？你的疑心病也太重了。我这里是个谜，谜底就是'针'，你想想是不是？"这一说，围观的人哄堂大笑，财主只好气得干瞪眼。这件事传了开去，据说就引出了"灯谜"的习俗，许多人都喜欢把谜语写在花灯上，让观灯的人猜测取乐。

An interesting legend about lantern riddles goes that once there was a rich man who usually bullied and oppressed the poor. A young man called Wang Shao became very angry and decided to take revenge on him on the night of the Lantern Festival by presenting him with a lantern bearing this riddle: "It is silver white, with the head sharp and body slight. / The hand of a scale hardly moves because its weight is too light./

On its tail are its eyes, / and only clothing not men can it recognize." The rich man was infuriated and ordered to take the lantern from Wang Shao, thinking that the riddle described him. Having taken his revenge, Wang Shao said, "What makes you think that it describes you? You are too suspicious. This is only a riddle and the answer is a needle. Think about it." Everyone laughed. The rich man could do nothing but stand by helplessly. The story spread quickly and it is now considered as the origin of lantern riddles. From then on, people like to put riddles on the lanterns for others to guess as a form of entertainment.

还有人说，正月十五挂红灯和农民起义领袖黄巢有关。那年，黄巢攻打浑城，一时之间攻不下，就化装成平民百姓进城去探个虚实。在城里，他差一点被官军抓住，幸亏有个老头救了他，还指点了攻城的诀窍。黄巢为了感激他，让他在正月十五夜挂个灯笼在门口。这个老头又把消息传给左邻右舍，不久城里的穷人都知道了，家家买红纸扎灯笼。后来，黄巢的军队在正月十五晚上攻进浑城，凡是挂红灯的人家都受到了保护。据说从此以后，就有了元宵挂灯的风俗。

Another legend says that the practice of hanging red lanterns has something to do with Huang Chao, leader of a peasant uprising. After he found that it was difficult to take the Huncheng City, Huang Chao entered the city in civilian disguise, trying to find out about the enemy. There he underwent a narrow escape with the help of an old man, who also told him about the strategies to take the city. In order to show his gratitude, Huang Chao told the old man to hang a lantern over his gate on the night of the Lantern Festival. Then the old man spread the news in the neighborhood and soon the poor people throughout the city began to make lanterns with red paper. Later, when Huang Chao's army took Huncheng City on the night of the Lantern Festival, those who had hung the lanterns were spared. Hence, the custom of hanging lanterns during the Lantern Festival came into being.

元宵节的掌故还有不少。据说宋朝有个州官，名叫田登，为了避"官讳"，不许老百姓说"登"字。因为"灯"和"登"同音，连"灯"字也不能写。元宵节官府贴出的告示居然被写成"本州依例，放火三日"。于是成为话柄，大家都说"只许州官放火，不许百姓点灯"，作为对于骄横跋扈者的绝妙讽刺。

There are many other legends about the festival. Once there was a governor called Tian Deng, who did not allow people to say the word "*deng*" in order to avoid the coincidental association with his own name. People were not even allowed to write the word "*deng* (lantern)" as it had the same pronunciation with his given name "*deng* (ascend)". Once before the Lantern Festival the local government put up a notice saying that "According to tradition, this prefecture will *fang huo* (set fire) for three days", deliberately avoiding the phrase *fang deng* (display lanterns). The story soon became a subject of ridicule. People all complained that a governor might commit arson while the governed were not allowed to light a lantern, ironically referring to the imperious and despotic rulers.

在迎灯的队伍里，最引人注目的往往是舞龙灯，又称为龙舞。

In the lantern parade, dragon-lantern dancing, also known as the dragon-dance, is usually the most eye-catching.

龙是十二生肖之一，与中华民族的历史文化有着极其密切的关系。大约在五千多年前的出土文物上，我们就已经发现了龙的形象。关于舞龙的文字记载，在汉代的文献中就已频频出现，可见它是由来已久的。古代以为，龙有呼风唤雨、消灾除疫的功能，是吉祥的象征，在节日庆典中舞龙很早就形成了习俗。较早出现的土龙，大概还不能舞动。后来又有了草龙，逐渐地就可以舞动起来。龙灯一般可分两大类，一类是可以点灯发亮的，主要在夜晚舞动；还有一种布龙，或称彩龙，则不燃蜡烛。两者各有千秋。前者往往是元宵夜一道奇特的风景线。江南一带有板凳龙，村里每户出一条板凳，其实它只是一条木板，板上由各户自己设计、制作一盏造型奇特的灯火，板的两头都有洞。舞龙时，村里出龙头、龙尾，每户人家的龙灯板就可以拼接上去，板与板拼接时用一根小木棒插入板上的小洞，犹如插销一般，再加上有人在旁护持，这样组成的板凳龙就可以舞动起来了。大的村落，往往会把板凳龙做成几百节长，在山路上蜿蜒前进，在广场上盘旋布阵，常常造成震撼人心的气势。

The dragon, one of the twelve Chinese zodiac animals, is an important part of Chinese culture and tradition. Some unearthed cultural relics, which existed more than 5,000 years ago, were decorated with sketches of dragons of a crude form. In ancient times, people thought that the dragon could make clouds and bring them rain and help them to avoid disasters and ward off illness. Therefore it was a symbol of prosperity and good luck. The dragon dances was frequently mentioned in the records of the Han Dynasty (206 BC — 220 AD) and has long been the Chinese custom during festivals ever since. Probably the earliest dragon — the earth dragon — could not dance at all, while the later grass dragon could. There are usually two kinds of dragon lanterns: a dragon with candle lights is called a lighted dragon, otherwise it is called a cloth dragon, or a colorful dragon. Though each has its merits, the lighted dragon dance, mainly performed at night is a real magnificent scene on the Lantern Festival. There is another one called the bench dragon to the south of the Yangtze River. Each household provides one bench, which is just a wooden board, with a specially-made light on it and holes on each end. All the benches are connected by a small stick, which functions as a bolt, into a whole, then the dragon's head and tail provided by the village are put on each end. With the dancer each holding up a stick in his section of the dragon, the bench dragon would begin to dance. A large village could make a bench dragon of hundreds of sections, which would wind through mountain roads and hover on squares, often a scene of excitement.

布龙不燃灯烛，因此可以在舞动的动作上出奇制胜，形成各种高难度的动作套路，令人眼花缭乱、啧啧称奇。

Without candle lights, the cloth dragon can display its highly skillful performance and extremely difficult tricks, which , to audiences, is so dazzling and intriguing.

说起龙灯，也有许多动人的传说。各个地方的人们通过自己的想象，解释龙灯的起源，虽然并非信史，却真切地流露出他们对历史的理解和对生活的态度。比如有的说，古时有一条老龙，不顾天帝的禁令，私自降雨，为民造福。后来天帝发现，将它杀死。百姓们为了纪念它，就做了条龙灯。每逢元宵节，就要舞龙灯。还有的说，有个灯匠，扎的龙灯特别奇妙。皇帝硬逼他扎龙灯。他的龙灯扎好了，龙也活了，居然把皇帝咬死，把皇宫烧掉，带着灯匠逃走了。

As for dragon lanterns, there are many moving stories.

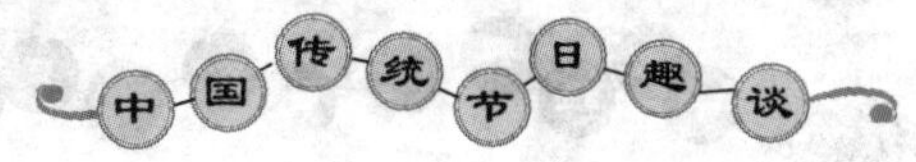

People tell stories about the origins of the dragon lantern out of imagination. Though the stories might not be true, they can vividly reveal our understanding about history and attitudes towards life. For instance, it is said that once an old dragon was killed after being found to have brought rain to help people without the permission of the Jade Emperor. People made dragon lanterns in memory of him, and performed dragon dances every Lantern Festival. It is also said that a lantern craftsman, famous for the wonderful lanterns he made, was forced to make a lantern for the emperor. When he finished, the dragon suddenly came alive and killed the emperor, burned the imperial palace down and flew away with the lantern craftsman.

元宵节吃汤圆，也是许多地方都流行的饮食风俗。汤圆又名"元宵"、"灯圆"，说明它与元宵灯节密不可分。这是一种用糯米粉做成的点心，中间有馅，或放肉，或放夹沙，放在水中煮熟。汤圆熟了之后，就会漂浮起来，犹如圆圆的月亮。天上月圆，碗里汤圆，再加上一家人团圆，这里有着极佳的象征意义，所以人人都喜爱它。台湾有首民歌《卖汤圆》，许多人都会唱："一碗汤圆满又满，吃了汤圆好团圆。"此情此景，令人向往。

Eating *tangyuan* (glutinous rice balls stuffed with either sweet or meat fillings) is also a tradition in many places. As its other names *yuanxiao* or *dengyuan* suggest, it is an

important part of the Lantern Festival. When boiled, *tangyuan* floats on the surface of the soup, like the full moon in the sky. People eat it as a symbol of family reunion. Family members get together, eating *tangyuan* and enjoying the full moon. It is so tasty that everyone likes it. Many people can sing the Taiwan folk song *Selling Tangyuan*, which goes like this, "The bowls are filled with *tangyuan*; after eating them families will enjoy reunion." Everyone will look forward to that moment.

许多少数民族也过元宵节，但活动内容则会有所变异。布依族过元宵节，有的地方要给祖坟亮灯，给祖先拜年；有的地方玩龙灯、跳狮子、舞花灯、放爆竹；有的地方还要放河灯。他们称元宵节之前是玩年期，元宵节以后，就开始下地劳动，或是出外谋生。在这一点上，其实许多汉族人也是如此，在许多地方，人们往往把过年的走亲戚、喝年酒一类的活动安排到元宵节为止。一过元宵节，就得好好去干活啦。说起来，这也是一种风俗。

Many ethnic groups in China also celebrate the Lantern Festival, but they have different customs. Take the Bouyei ethnic group for an example. In some places people light candles in their ancestors' graveyards and offer sacrifices; in other places dragon dances, lion dances, lantern displays and fireworks are popular; it is traditional for people to put paper lamps in the river. For them the Spring Festival comes to an end when the Lantern Festival is over. They will start work on the farm or in far-away cities. The same is true with the Han people. Their activities like visiting friends and having dinner parties end on the day of the Lantern Festival. It is conventional for people to start work afterwards.

三、二月二

3. The Double-Second Festival

二月二，又称“花朝节”、“踏青节”、“挑菜节”，俗称“龙抬头日”。大约在唐代就已形成。白居易有《二月二日》诗：“二月二日新雨晴，草芽菜甲一时生。轻衫细马春年少，十字津头一字行。”在这一天，民间相互送礼，还有挑菜、迎富、踏青等活动。明代以后，又有撒灰引龙的习俗，称为“龙抬头”。

The Double-Second Festival (or the Spring Dragon Festival) is traditionally named the Dragon Head Festival, which is also called “the Day of Legendary Birth of Flowers”, “the Spring Outing Day”, or “the Vegetables-Picking Day”. It came into existence in the Tang Dynasty (618 AD—907 AD). The poet, Bai Juyi wrote a poem entitled *The Second Day of the Second Lunar Month*: “The first rain stops, sprout grass and vegetables. In light clothes are young lads, and in lines as they cross the streets.” On this special day, people send gifts to each other, pick vegetables, welcome wealth and go on a spring outing, etc. After the Ming Dynasty (1368 AD—1644 AD), the custom of spreading ashes to attract a dragon was called “dragon lifting its head”.

为什么叫“龙抬头”呢？北方民间有这么一个传说。

Why is it called “dragon lifting its head”? There is a folktale in northern China.

说是有一年，玉帝传谕四海龙王，三年内不得向人间降雨。一时间民不聊生，百姓苦不堪言。有一条玉龙不忍心了，就私自向人间下了一场透雨。这事很快被玉帝发觉，便把玉龙打下凡间，压在一座大山下受罪。山上立了块碑，说是除非金豆开花，玉龙才能重新上天。

It is said that once the Jade Emperor ordered the four Sea Dragon Kings not to rain on the earth in three years’ time. At a time, life for the people was intolerable and the people suffered untold misery and hardship. One of the four Dragon Kings — the jade dragon was sympathetic with the people and secretly dropped a soaking rain on the earth, which was soon discovered by the Jade Emperor, who banished him to the mortal world and put him under a huge mountain. On it was a tablet, which said the jade dragon would not go back to Heaven unless golden beans blossomed.

老百姓知道了，奔走相告，大家都在想办法要拯救玉龙。一天，一个老婆婆背了一袋玉米，上街去卖，不小心袋口松开，金黄金黄的玉米籽撒了满地。人们心头一亮，心想，玉米籽不就是金豆吗，炒炒不就开花了吗？于是大家齐心协力，约定在二月二这天，家家炒玉米花，放在庭院里。太白金星人老眼花，一看，果然是金豆开花了，就把玉龙给放了出来。

People went around telling the news and were thinking of ways to save the dragon. One day, an old woman carried a sack of corn for sale on the street. The sack opened and the golden corn scattered on the ground. It occurred to people that seeds of corn were the gold beans, which would blossom if they were roasted. Therefore, people coordinated their efforts to roast popcorn and place it in the yards on the second day of the second lunar month. The God Venus had dim eyesight with old age. He was under the impression that golden beans blossomed, so he released the dragon.

从此以后，民间便有了这个风俗，每年二月二这天，家家户户都要炒玉米花。有的还边炒边唱："二月二，龙抬头，大仓满，

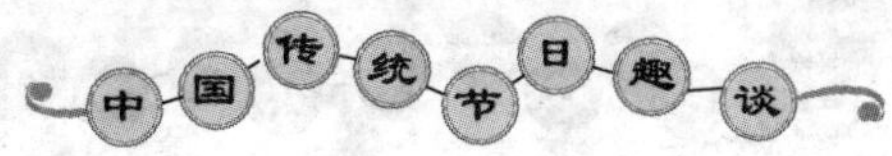

小仓流。”

From then on there was a custom on the earth that on the second day of the second lunar month, every family would roast popcorn. Some people sang while roasting: “The dragon lifts its head on the second day of the second lunar month. Large barns will be full and small ones will overflow.”

聚居在红河南岸哀牢山中的哈尼族，则把二月二当做“祭龙日”，这一带民间传颂着两个勇敢的小伙子诛杀恶魔，为百姓除害的动人故事。

While the Hani ethnic group inhabiting in Mount Ailao on the southern bank of the Red River referred to this day as the Day of Worshipping Dragons, with a moving folktale of two brave young men slaughtering a demon.

人们又把二月二叫做花朝节。也有些地方把二月十二，或是二月十五叫做花朝节的。总之，意思是说春天快要到了，百花又要争相开放了。人们以为掌管百花的花神应该是有生日的，她的生日就应该在春天，于是就把某一天定做“百花生日”。民间说是百花生日，到了文人嘴里，说得雅一些，就成了花朝节。

The festival is also known as the Day of the Legendary Birth of Flowers, which falls on the 12th or 15th of the second lunar month in some other places. Since spring is around the corner and all flowers will soon be in bloom, the day is set as

the birthday of the Flower God, which is believed to be in spring. It later gets an elegant name of the Day of the Legendary Birth of Flowers from men of letters.

这一天，往往有赏花、种花、踏青和赏红等一系列活动。旧时，在许多地方都还有花神庙，于是就要在这一天祭祀花神。人们用红的纸带、布条系在花枝上，称为“赏红”。还有以这一天的阴晴来占卜全年小麦、花果丰歉的俗信。

A series of activities are held on this day, including appreciating flowers, growing flowers, going on a spring outing, and attaching red straps to branches. Sacrifices are offered to the Flower God at Flower God Temples in many places. Red straps of paper or cloth are tied to the stems of flowers. The weather that day is seen as the divination of a year’s yield of wheat, flowers and fruits.

壮族同胞把二月二叫做“百花仙子节”，每年这天，男女青年都要聚集在长有木棉树的平坝对歌。对歌中必定有歌颂百花仙子的内容。他们还要抛绣球，互赠礼物。得到绣球的青年会把绣球挂到木棉树上。人们以为，百花仙子就住在木棉树上，他们用这种办法祈求百花仙子保佑爱情常红，心地洁白。

People of the Zhuang ethnic group name it the Day of Hundred-Flower Fairy. Youngsters will gather around a dam with bombax trees, singing a musical dialogue in antiphonal style, throwing embroidered balls to their loves and exchanging gifts. They will sing songs worshipping the Hundred-Flower Fairy. The embroidered balls they get will be hung on the bombax trees, where the Hundred-Flower Fairy is believed to live in. In this way, the Hundred-Flower Fairy will bless them with pure and sweet love forever.

江南的花果农要给果树做生日。旧时的这一天，妇女们会将果园的杂草锄掉，在每棵果树四周松土。中午时分，在一棵棵树干上贴一方红纸，再用稻草捆住，树枝叉处压一块石头，然后双手扶着果树，轻轻叨念："桃子今年多吗？多的！桃子今年大吗？大的！桃子今年蛀吗？不蛀！桃子今年脱吗？不脱！"念毕，举起小竹刀，在树干中部不轻不重地斫上一刀。如此这般，一棵棵果树轮着都这么做一遍。也可以是两人配合着，一问一答，一人代表主人，一人代表果树。这里似乎还可以窥见远古时代巫术残存的痕迹，不过时至今日，恐怕也只是在表达果农们的一种心愿罢了。据专家说，果农们在果树上不轻不重地斫上这么一刀，却是蛮有些科学依据的。果树如果长势过旺，果实容易脱落；倘若恰到好处地斫上一刀，恰恰可以起到"回滋"的作用，有利于果树结实。由此可见，保存在民众中的一些知识，其实很是宝贵。

It is also considered as the birthday of the fruit trees in the south of Yangtze River. Women used to hoe up weeds and loosen the soil around each tree. At noon, a piece of red paper

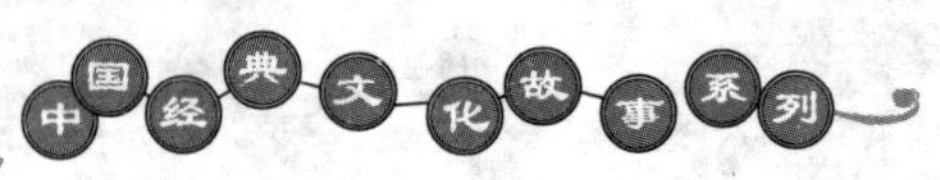

would be pasted on the trunk of each tree, and then people would cover it with straw. A stone was put on the crotch. People would put both hands on the tree, whispering "Will there be a good harvest of peaches? Yes! Will peaches be big? Yes! Will peaches be moth-eaten? No! Will peaches drop? No!" Then they would lift a bamboo knife and cut the middle part of the trunk with moderate strength. The process was repeated for each fruit tree and could be carried out with the joint effort of two people, with one asking the questions, representing the host, and the other answering the questions, standing for the tree. It was originally a form of the ancient witchcraft, and is now only a good wish of the fruit growers. According to the experts, to cut the tree with moderate strength has its scientific foundation. If the growing of the trees is too fast, fruits tend to drop. The cutting has the function of "retaining nutrition", to help to bear fruits, which shows that some knowledge from the populace is precious.

四、三月三

3. The Double-Third Festival

“三月三”这个节日，不但在汉族地区流行，也还在许多少数民族地区盛传不衰。有人认为它就是古代的上巳节。古时以夏历三月的第一个巳日为“上巳”。有人说起于周公曲水之宴，有人说起于周时的水滨祓禊，总之，这是一个十分古老的节日。古人在这一天，要到水边去举行祭祀仪式，用香薰草药沐浴，以祓除污渍与秽气。再是在野外或水边招魂续魄，既是召唤亲人的亡魂，也是召唤自己的魂魄苏醒。不难看出，这里充满着古老的巫术。不过在这样一种巫术仪式结束之后，却总是会展开青年男女春游和谈情说爱的生动场景，让人流连忘返。这种场景，在《诗经》中就有过形象的描述。

The Double-Third Festival is popular for both the Han people and many other ethnic groups. As for its origin, one story says that the Double-Third Festival was exactly the ancient Shangsi Festival, which was on the first si day of the third month in the Chinese lunar calendar in ancient times. Some said that it came from the Dinner Party at the Qushui River of the Zhou Dynasty (1046 BC—221 BC). Others said that it came down from the custom of a ceremony to get rid of the evils by bathing in the river. Whatever it was, it was an old festival, on which people would hold a sacrificing ceremony on the riverside to honor their ancestors, and then take a bath in the river with herbs to get rid of the filth from their bodies. Or people would have evocation to call back the spirits, the spirits of their deceased relatives, or to make their own spirits come to themselves, which was, of course, full of ancient sorcery. However, what followed this ceremony is really attractive — young men and women would go for a spring outing and romance, and its wonderful scene was vividly described in *Shi Jing* (*The Book of Songs*).

上巳节的活动内容，历代都有变化。汉代又增加了临水宴宾和求子。魏晋以后，上巳改为三月三。东晋书法家王羲之的《兰亭集序》，记载了当时的文人墨客在绍兴兰亭修禊，吟诗饮酒，曲水流觞的风流雅事，这是许多人都熟知的掌故。唐代，每逢此节，皇帝要在曲江大宴群臣，民间男女也喜欢到水边饮宴游玩，长安一带还有斗百草游戏。明清以后，祓禊逐渐淡出，衍变为春游，民间有流杯、流卵、流枣、乞子、戴柳圈、探春、踏青、吃青粳饭、举行歌会等活动内容，生活气息十分浓郁。又由于上巳的时间与清明相近，后来便与清明节合而为一。今天的许多青年人则已经只知道清明节而不知道上巳节了。

The activities of the Shangsi Festival have varied with times. The entertainment feast and praying for descendants along the riverside were added in the Han Dynasty (206 BC — 220 AD). It was after the Wei and Jin dynasties (220 AD — 420 AD) that the Shangsi Festival developed into the Double-Third Festival. The calligrapher Wang Xizhi in the Eastern Jin Dynasty (317 AD — 420 AD) recorded in his *Preface to the Collection of Lanting Poems* about how those men of pen took a bath to get rid of filth and how they chanted poems while drinking from the drifting cups along the winding river. These well-known stories have become literary anecdotes in history. Whenever this festival came in the Tang Dynasty (618 AD — 907 AD), the emperor would feast all his followers beside the river while the people, both men and women, would enjoy drinking, going sight-seeing or cricket-fighting as practiced in the area of the City of Chang'an, along the river. After the Ming and Qing dynasties (1368 AD — 1911 AD), the practice of taking a bath to get rid of filth gradually developed into a spring outing which was featured with lively activities like drifting cups, drifting eggs, drifting dates, throwing-stone, wearing willow-wreath, exploring for spring, hiking, having glutinous rice and antiphonal. As the Shangsi Festival is very close in time to the Clear-and-Bright Festival, it later merged with the latter in many regions. As a result, many young people today only know something about the Clear-and-Bright Festival but have no idea about the Shangsi Festival.

而在一部分地区，又有三月节或三月会的习惯，究其时间，也总是在三月三。

In some regions there has been a custom of observing the Third Lunar Month Festival or the Third Lunar Month Fair, which is always held on the third day of the third lunar month.

在四川忠县一带，则流传着一则感人肺腑的传说。战国时，巴蔓子是川东巴国将领，当时邻国入侵，求楚国相助，楚国出兵获胜后，要挟巴国要送给楚国三座城池。为了保护城池，巴蔓子割颈自刎。楚国大为震撼，不得不退了兵。当地百姓十分感激巴蔓子，为他立了个庙，叫做土主庙。三月三是他自刎的日子，每年这一天，人们都要抬着巴蔓子的神像绕城游行，隆重纪念他。家家张灯结彩，燃放爆竹，人们都用这样一种方式来纪念这位了不起的英雄。

A moving legend was often told around the area of Zhongxian County, Sichuan Province. It was about a famous Ba general, Bamanzi, in Eastern Sichuan. At the time of the invasion by a neighboring state, the Ba State had to ask for military help from the Chu State. But after they won the battle, the Chu State asked the Ba State to give it three cities in return. To preserve these cities, Bamanzi killed himself by cutting his neck with a sword. Shocked by his death, the Chu State withdrew its army. The local people built a temple named Tuzhu Temple to show their gratitude and respect for Bamanzi. As he died on the third day of the third lunar month, people would hang up lanterns, set off firecrackers and carry Bamanzi's portrait in a parade around the city in honor of this great hero on this day of the year.

三月三，同时又是我国南方许多少数民族的传统节日，流行在壮、侗、布依、水、仫佬、毛南、苗、瑶、畲等民族中间。

In South China, the Double-Third Festival is also a traditional festival among many ethnic minorities like Zhuang, Dong, Bouyei, Shui, Oroqen, Maonan, Miao, Yao and She.

壮族，一般在这天赶歌圩，搭歌棚，举办歌会，让青年男女对歌、碰蛋、抛绣球，谈情说爱。传说壮族历史上有位歌仙刘三姐，又称刘三妹。她擅长歌唱，三位秀才来对歌，都败在她手下。后来她骑着鲤鱼上了天，在广西一带留下不少佳话。后人纪念她，把三月三叫做“歌仙节”。

On the third day of the third lunar month every year, the Zhuang ethnic group will gather in the open to set up a singing tent and take part in a singing party, where young men and women sing in antiphonal style, bump eggs, throw embroidered balls, and express their love to each other. There was once a Zhuang girl called Liu Sanjie (Third Sister Liu), who was very good at singing and even defeated three young men with her witty singing, according to the legend. She later went up to Heaven on the back of a carp and became the Singing Goddess. To honor her, people gave another name to the third day of the third lunar month, “the Singing Goddess Day”.

侗族，多在这天抢花炮、斗牛、斗鸟、对歌、踩堂，又称“花炮节”。

The Dong ethnic group calls the Double-Third Festival “Firework-Scrambling Festival”, when people compete for firework-scrambling (a round, iron ring, 5 cm in diameter with red cloth or silk twined around it), go for bull-fighting or bird-fighting, sing in antiphonal style and have *caitang* dances.

布依族，在这天杀猪祭社神、山神，吃黄色糯米饭，各个村寨之间，好几天不相往来。

On the day of the Double-Third Festival, the Bouyei ethnic group would busy themselves with celebrating the worship of the mountain and community gods with pigs and steaming glutinous rice, too busy to visit the neighboring villages for several days.

瑶、黎、水、畲等各个民族也都有他们自己独特的节俗，我们无法一一细说，不过从中传达出来的节日情怀，却是相通的。

Other ethnic groups like the Miao, Yao and She, usually hold various activities rich in ethnic flavor, which cannot be mentioned one by one, but their festival atmosphere is the same.

五、清明节

5. The Clear-and-Bright Festival

民间有“清明大如年”的说法，可见人们是把它当做一个大节日来过的。其实，清明是二十四节气中的一个节气。说清明，就必须先说说二十四节气。

There has long been a saying that the Clear-and-Bright Festival (or the Pure Brightness Festival) is as important as the Spring Festival, which shows how important this festival is. In fact, Clear-and-Bright is only a solar term, one of the 24 seasonal division terms in China. So one cannot talk about Clear-and-Bright without mentioning the 24 seasonal division terms first.

古人根据太阳在黄道上的位置变化和地面气候演变的次序，将全年划分为二十四个段落，每段相隔半个月。大约到了秦汉的时候，二十四节气就已完全确立，并且成为农事活动的主要依据了。民间流传着大量的谚语，告诉人们什么节气该干什么农活，很清楚。二十四节气并不都是节日，不过其中的立春、清明、立夏、立秋、冬至，历来也总是把它们当做节日来过的。时至今日，其他一些节气大多淡出人们的记忆，独有清明，却盛传不衰，成为我国传统节日中的佼佼者。

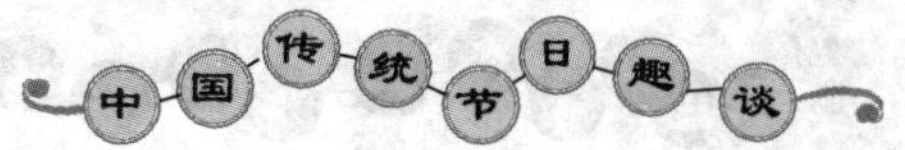

According to the changing positions of the sun in the elliptic and seasonal changes of climate on the earth, the traditional Chinese calendar divides a year into 24 solar terms at the interval of 15 days. These 24 solar terms were completely established around the Qin and Han dynasties (221 BC — 220 AD), and have become the basis for agricultural activities ever since. A large number of proverbs have been popular among folks telling people what specific agricultural activities they should do during different solar seasons. Not all the 24 solar seasons are considered to be festivals. But some of them, like the Beginning of Spring, Clear-and-Bright, the Beginning of Summer, the Beginning of Autumn and Winter Solstice, are usually observed as festivals. While many other solar seasons leave no traces on people's minds, the Clear-and-Bright Festival occupies an outstanding position among the Chinese traditional festivals.

清明在夏历三月间，公历四月五日前后。清明节的活动，在今天主要是踏青、扫墓、植树等内容。而在历史上，清明节的内容则比今天多得多，这里也有一个逐渐衍变的过程。

The Clear-and-Bright Festival occurs in the third lunar month and around the fifth of April. Activities like going hiking, sweeping tombs and planting trees are what people often do during the festival. However, there were much more

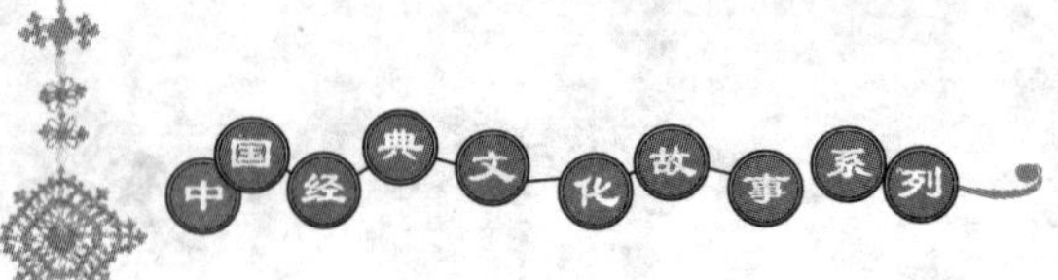

activities in ancient times than what we have today, from which we can trace the course of a gradual evolution.

说清明总要先从寒食说起。古代，清明的前一两天，还有个寒食节。这一天禁用烟火，人们只好冷食，所以称为寒食。古诗有“未到清明先禁火”，说的就是这种习俗。

The Clear-and-Bright Festival developed out of the Cold-Food Festival. In ancient times, the Cold-Food Festival was usually one or two days before the Clear-and-Bright Festival. It got its name from the custom of eating cold food because of the fire-forbidding practice on that day. “Prohibiting fire before the Clear-and-Bright Festival comes” is a line from an ancient poem, which demonstrates the observance of this custom.

为什么要禁火呢？这里有个传说。

Why is the fire forbidden? It originated from a legend.

春秋时，晋文公重耳在执政前曾经一度流亡在外，吃过不少苦。有个介子推，一直忠心耿耿跟随着他。有一次，介子推甚至割下自己腿上的一块肉来给重耳吃。后来，重耳登上王位，大封功臣，却偏偏把介子推给忘记了。介子推心里不是滋味，也不明说，背着他的老母亲躲进了深山。

It was about Jie Zitui who lived in the Spring and Autumn

Period (770 BC — 476 BC). Before Chong're (Duke Wen) was in power, he had been forced to go into exile, and Jie Zitui bore the misery together with him and followed him faithfully all the way. On one occasion, he even cut his own flesh from his leg and boiled it for hungry Chong'er. But when Chong'er became the monarch and granted titles to his meritorious followers, he forgot Jie Zitui. Sad and disappointed in heart, Jie Zitui said nothing and went to live in seclusion with his mother in the mountains.

后来，有人在晋文公面前提起了介子推；也有的说是介子推自己写了首诗《龙蛇之歌》，讽刺晋文公，这诗让晋文公看到了。总之，后来晋文公发觉自己亏待了介子推，要去找介子推补救，却已经找不到他了。晋文公派御林军进山去搜索，这时候有人急于求成，竟放火烧山，以为这样一来，介子推就会不得不逃出来。谁知道介子推很倔，竟抱着一棵树，让大火活活烧死，却就是不肯出来。据说介子推死在山西介休县的山里，后来山西一带的民众为了纪念他，在他的忌辰，禁火一个月，后来又改为禁火三天，相沿成俗，这就是寒食节的由来。人们因为禁火，需要重新用榆柳取火，所以就在门口插柳。人们还用柳条穿着面粉做成“子推燕”，挂在门口，为介子推母子招魂。这个习俗后来就演变为门前插柳条，或是在头上戴柳圈，或是在鬓边插柳，俗信以为可以驱毒、明眼、祈年，这都已经是后来的事了。

There are different versions about what happened later.

According to one version, someone happened to mention Jie Zitui to Duke Wen one day. The other version says that it was the satirical poem *The Song of Dragon and Snake* written by Jie Zitui, that was presented to Duke Wen. Whichever version was true, its consequence was that Duke Wen realized that he had treated Jie Zitui shabbily. To make up for his mistake, he went to look for Jie Zitui but in vain. Then he sent his palace guards to search for Jie Zitui in the mountains. During the search, someone was so anxious for success as to set fire to the mountains, thinking that the fire would surely drive Jie Zitui out of the mountains. Out of everyone's expectations, Jie Zitui was such an obstinate person that he would rather be burnt to death than go out. It was said that Jie Zitui died with a tree in his arms in the mountains in the Jiexiu County, Shanxi Province. To commemorate him, the Shanxi people would not light fire from the day Jie Zitui died for a month, which was later shortened to three days. This practice gradually developed into a custom, which is the origin of the Cold-Food Festival. As fire was forbidden, people had to return to the elm willow for starting fire. Therefore, they planted willow trees in front of their gates. Willow branches were also used to make "Zitui Swallows" by piercing the branches through the dough. People hung these "Zitui Swallows" at the gates to call back the spirit of Jie Zitui and his mother. This custom gradually involves activities like plugging willow branches in front of the gates, wearing willow wreath and sticking a willow twig in one's sideburns, for the folks believe that this can rid them of illness, make clear their eyes and bless them with a good harvest, which is the later story.

也有人指出，其实早在周朝就已经有暮春禁火的记载了，恐怕把寒食与介子推之死联系在一起的说法经不起推敲。不过。作为民间传说，这个故事表达了民众对于历史的一种评介，尽管有些附会，也还是颇为珍贵的。

As someone pointed out, the fire-forbidden practice at the end of spring was actually recorded as early as the Zhou Dynasty (1046 BC—221 BC). Therefore, it sounds dubious when people connect the death of Jie Zitui with the practice of eating cold food. Anyhow, the legend is a valuable expression of people's review on history though they may be a little farfetched.

因为寒食和清明的日子相隔很近，渐渐地，人们把寒食的节日活动延续到了清明。前面提到，这段时间里还有个上巳节，是以祓禊招魂、踏青郊游为主要特征的。这种活动后来也被融合进了清明。一般认为，从唐代开始，清明才成为一个重要节日，它的节日活动里就包括了寒食、上巳的许多内容。

Because of the adjacency of the Cold-Food Festival and

the Clear-and-Bright Festival in time, people gradually extended the activities of the Cold-Food Festival till the Clear-and-Bright Festival. As is mentioned above, there used to be the Shangsi Festival during this time, which is featured with offering sacrifices to get ride of disasters and beg blessings, call back the spirit of the dead as well as go hiking. These activities later merged into those of the Clear-and-Bright Festival. Generally speaking, it was from the Tang Dynasty (618 AD — 907 AD) that the Clear-and-Bright Festival became an important one, which included many activities of the Cold-Food Festival and the Shangsi Festival.

在二十四节气里，清明的本意是说这时候春天到了，万物开始生长，农忙也即将来临，提醒人们不要忘记农事。不过作为传统节日，它的主要内容还是祭扫祖坟和踏青游春。而这两件事，在从前往往又是连在一起的。唐代大诗人白居易的诗："乌鹊噪昏乔木，清明寒食谁家哭，风吹旷野纸钱飞，古墓累累春草绿。"就是对当年清明节风俗的生动写照。

Among the 24 solar seasons, Clear-and-Bright originally refers to, and aims to remind people of the time when spring begins, when everything begins to grow and when the busy season for farming approaches. However, as a traditional festival, it mainly includes sweeping their family tombs and going for spring outings. The great poet Bai Juyi in the Tang

Dynasty (618 AD—907 AD) vividly depicted the observance of the Clear-and-Bright Festival in one of his poems:

"With the crowing of birds in the woods
comes the weeping of tomb-sweepers;
In the wind of the Clear-and-Bright Festival,
flies the spirit money above the green tombs."

饮水思源，慎终追远，这是中华民族的传统美德。历史上，大多数地区沿袭土葬，人们对祖坟都很看重。每年清明节，家家户户都要到祖坟上去祭奠一番，带去一些酒食果品作为供奉，在坟前烧些纸钱，虔诚叩拜，表示对祖先的悼念。还要为坟墓除草培土，在坟上插几枝新柳，或是种几株新树，以示养护。扫墓之后，人们便会找一个地方，把祭奠先人的酒食果品吃掉，这就有些像今天的野餐了。

Paying tribute to our ancestors is one of the Chinese virtues. As it is a traditional practice for people in many places to bury the dead in the ground, they attach great importance to their family tombs. Therefore, on the day of the Clear-and-Bright Festival every year, people visit their family graveyards, holding memorial ceremonies, presenting wine and fruits as sacrifice, burning spirit money, and kowtowing piously to their ancestors. Besides, weeds are pulled, new earth is covered on the tombs, and new branches of willow or young trees are planted around the tombs. After this, people will find a place to eat up the food they laid out in front of the grave, which is just like today's picnic.

坟墓都在郊外，住在城里的居民到郊外扫墓，事实上也就是一次郊游。这个时候风和日丽，莺飞草长，到处勃勃生机，自然而然会引发人们踏青的情绪。清明踏青，大约在宋代就已蔚然成风。著名的《清明上河图》，就是宋朝时节汴京人民踏青远足的风俗画，文人诗词的歌咏自然就更多了。所谓踏青，用今天的话来说，也就是休闲旅游的一种样式，这也是不言而喻的。

As the graveyards are located in the suburbs, going to sweep tombs is, in the eyes of urban citizens, to go hiking. Bathing in the warm sunshine, with birds singing and grass growing everywhere, the lively nature arouses the enthusiasm of spring outings on this day. Since the Song Dynasty (960 AD — 1279 AD), people have followed the custom of spring outings. The famous painting *Along the River During the Clear-and-Bright Festival* vividly depicts the spring outings of the Bianjing people in the Song Dynasty. And it is natural for people to write poems and songs about it. Of course, going for an outing today is a relaxing tour.

清明踏青，又势必会引出许多游艺活动，诸如荡秋千、放风筝、驰马、蹋球、斗鸡、拔河以及名目繁多、花样翻新的游戏，往往会使人心旷神怡，乐而忘返。也许有人会问，不是说清明节的主要活动是祭扫祖坟吗？人们都应该在悲哀之中才是，怎么一会儿工夫就又嘻嘻哈哈起来了呢？这也不难解释。中华民族对于生死的理解其实是很豁达的，一般认为人的生命出自黄土而又回归黄土，这是一种循环。历来把老人高寿而又在自己家里去世称之为“寿终正寝”，把为这样的人办丧事称之为“白喜事”，活着的人并不会过于悲伤，而是以为逝者很平安地走完了他的人生之路，值得欣慰。每年清明节扫墓，则是为了表达对逝者的孝敬和思念。在仪式之后，放松一下心情，是很正常的一种需求。再则，旧时的女子很少出门，尤其是很少到郊外，她们借此机会来到旷野之中，这种喜悦之情就会比男子更加强烈。同时我们还要指出，清明踏青是继承了上巳遗风，这样一种在春天的野外狂欢的传统，其实也是由来已久了。

Spring outings during the Clear-and-Bright Festival are enjoyed together with many other carefree and joyous games, such as swinging, kite flying, horse riding, ball kicking, rooster fighting and tugs of war. Some might feel puzzled about what has turned this tomb sweeping event into such a joyous occasion. Actually, it is not difficult to understand that. For one thing, the Chinese people hold an open-minded view towards death. They consider it a natural circle that people born out of earth have to return to it after death. The death of those in a venerable age is called “a natural death”, and the funeral for this person is called a “white happiness” because they think that it is a good thing for a person to finish his/her

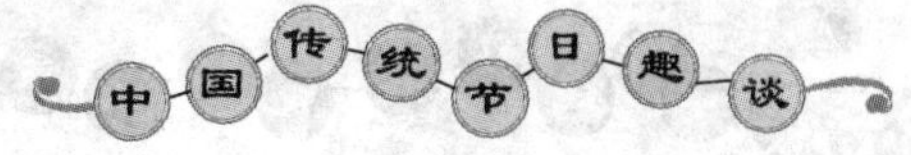

life peacefully in bed and that it is unnecessary for people to be too sad about it. Sweeping tombs on the Clear-and-Bright Festival is to show filial respect for the dead and it is quite natural for tomb-sweepers to have a rest and relaxation after the ceremony. For another, in the old days, there were very few occasions for women to go out of their houses, especially to the suburbs. Therefore, going out to sweep the tombs became rare and happy opportunities for women to enjoy themselves in nature, and the happiness it brought to them was much stronger than that to men. We must bear in mind that it was from the Shangsi Festival that the Clear-and-Bright Festival inherited the tradition of spring outings, so the tradition of enjoyable out-of-door activities in spring really has a long history.

清明节的食俗也很别致。这或许与寒食节有关。古时寒食节禁火，人们不得不预先准备一些食品，以供节日里冷食。后来，风俗演变，清明节不再禁火，但是当初一些饮食的传统习俗却保留了下来。用今天的话来说，清明节的点心小吃就比较引人注目，各地又往往会别出心裁，形成各自的地方小吃。

The food of the Clear-and-Bright Festival is very special. It has something to do with the Cold-Food Festival. In ancient times, people had to prepare some food in advance for the coming Clear-and-Bright Festival. Later on, though the Cold-

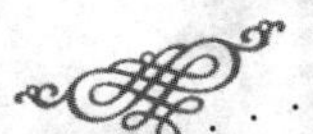

Food Festival was not so strictly observed as days went on, some of the food tradition remained. That is why the Clear-and-Bright snacks are so special and so characteristic of local flavors.

汉魏六朝时，流行在寒食节吃粥，这在《荆楚岁时记》里就有记载。一直到明代，还有在这一天吃桃花粥的习俗，采来新鲜桃花，配上好米熬粥，别有一番风味。

During the Han, Wei and Six Dynasties, porridge was a popular food for the Cold-Food Festival, which was recorded in Jingchu Suishiji (*Festivals in the Jingchu Area*). The custom lasted till the Ming Dynasty (1368 AD — 1644 AD) when people picked fresh peach flowers to make, mixed with quality rice, flavorous peach-blossom porridge.

南方有吃青粳饭的习俗。把杨桐叶、细冬青的叶子采来捣成汁，烧在饭里，饭就成了青色，据说这种饭特别滋补。后来，这种习俗又有所演变，许多地方都流行起青团子来。从野外采集一种嫩草，捣烂挤压成汁，揉入糯米粉，做成团子，再放入馅，上笼蒸熟，就成了可口的青团子。

In the south, it is customary to have “green rice” on that day, which is made of rice mixed with juice from the poplar tung leaves and narrow holly leaves. It is said that this “green rice” is very nutritious. Later, this custom underwent some changes. People squeeze juice from a particular kind of wild grass, mix it with rice and turn it into a round ball. Then they put some mince into the ball and steam it well. Thus, the delicious green ball is ready for you.

各地又有清明节吃馓子的习俗，南方用米面做，北方用麦面做，成形后放入油锅炸，香脆可口，古称“寒具”，看来也是寒食遗风。

Fried dough twists are also the traditional food for the festival. Rice powder as used in the south or wheat powder as used in the north is made into different shapes and then fried in the hot oil into delicious crisp fried dough twists. They are called “cold provisions”, a name closely related to the Cold-Food Festival.

有的地方喜欢在清明节吃蛋。鸡蛋煮熟后，用茜草汁在蛋壳上描绘花卉，几天后就渗进蛋壳，再把壳剥去，蛋白上便会显现可爱的图案，十分别致。在绘蛋的基础上，后来又出现了雕蛋，那就是一种民间工艺品了。在江南水乡，还有清明祭祖，阖家团聚，吃“清明夜饭”的习俗，那就有些像过年了。凡此种种，我们似乎都可以从中窥见古老节俗所留下的依稀印痕。而清明植树，其实也是传统的沿袭，只是古人只在祖坟植树，而今则扩大了范围。绿化环境，保护生态，如今已经成为全球的共识。从这个意义上说，清明节也就愈加值得我们珍惜了。

In some places, boiled eggs are the favorite food for the festival. People would paint some flowers on the boiled eggs with rubia cordifolia juice. Several days later, when the shell is stripped, lovely, delicate patterns will be seen on the egg white. Based on the egg-painting skills, a folk craft, egg-carving, appeared later. In the regions south of the Yangtze River, people sweep tombs and enjoy the family reunion with a "Clear-and-Bright dinner", just in the same way as what they do the Spring Festival. All the above-mentioned activities are vaguely impressed with the customs from those old festivals. Planting trees during the Clear-and-Bright Festival is also an example of this tradition. It used to be a custom to plant a few new trees around the family graves, but nowadays people tend to plant trees in a larger area. Protecting our ecological environment has gained global awareness and attention. In this sense, the Clear-and-Bright Festival is becoming a more significant festival for us.

六、端午节

6. The Double-Fifth Festival

端午节在农历五月初五，又称“重午”、“端阳”、“天中节”、“夏节”、“龙船节”……据说有二十多种叫法。古人有个习惯，喜欢把月和日的数字重复的这一天作为节日，除了正月初一之外，二月二、三月三、六月六、七月七、九月九，就都是节日。在这些重日节日里，端午是被人们特别看重的。

Falling on the fifth day of the fifth lunar month, the Double-Fifth Festival, also known as the Duanwu Festival, has more than 20 alternative Chinese names—the Chongwu Festival, the Duanyang Festival, the Tianzhong Festival, the Summer Festival, the Dragon-Boat Festival, etc. It is a practice for the ancient Chinese to choose the same number of the day and of the month for a festival. Apart from the first day of the first lunar month, which is the Spring Festival, we have the second day of the second lunar month as the Double-Second Festival, the third day of the third lunar month as the Double-Third Festival, the seventh day of the seventh lunar month as the Double-Seventh Festival and the ninth day of the ninth lunar month as the Double-Ninth Festival. And they are all important Chinese festivals, among which the Double-Fifth

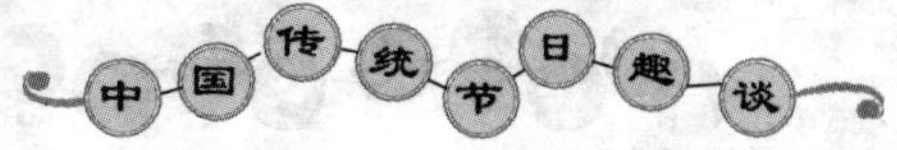

Festival is the most significant.

关于端午节的起源，历来众说纷纭，莫衷一是，学者们加以归纳，至少也有十种不同说法。这中间，影响最大的，大概是纪念屈原的说法。

There are various versions about the origin of the Double-Fifth Festival, and at least ten different ones are sorted out by scholars, among which the most influential version is to honor Qu Yuan.

屈原是战国时代的楚国诗人，官居三闾大夫。起初，楚怀王很重用他。后来楚怀王偏信奸臣进谗，没有接受屈原联齐抗秦的主张，反倒被骗到秦国，死在异乡。楚顷襄王又不思振复，将屈原削职放逐，长期流浪在沅湘流域。后来楚国首都郢被秦兵攻破，屈原救国的愿望无法实现，在极度悲愤之中，投汨罗江而死。传说屈原投江就是在农历五月初五，那天，楚国人民纷纷划船去救，在江上来回打捞他的尸体，有人还拿出粽子，丢到江中，说是让鱼虾吃了，它们就不会去咬屈大夫的尸体了。有个老医生拿了一坛雄黄酒倒进江里，说是要药晕蛟龙，别让它伤害屈大夫。后来水面上果然浮起一条蛟龙，龙须上还沾着一片屈大夫的衣襟，人们把这条恶龙拖上岸，斩头抽筋，把龙筋缠在小孩的手上、脖子上，据说毒蛇害虫也就不敢伤害小孩了。

It is said that Qu Yuan was a poet, and a minister in the State of Chu during the Warring States Period (475 BC —

221 BC). At first he won the full confidence and respect of his sovereign, King Huai of the Chu State. But later the king was surrounded by jealous self-seekers, so he ignored Qu Yuan's claim that the State of Chu ought to unite with the State of Qi to fight against the State of Qin. As a result, King Huai was tricked into the State of Qin and died there. King Qingxiang of Chu, the eldest son of King Huai, didn't take revenge, but dismissed Qu Yuan from office and sent him into exile as a vagrant in the Yuanxiang Valley (area around the present-day Yuanjiang River and Xiangjiang River in Hunan Province). Later the capital of Chu was captured by the troops from Qin. In great agony, Qu Yuan drowned himself in the Milo River with his wishes to save his beloved country unfulfilled. One legend claims that the day when Qu Yuan drowned himself in the river was the fifth day of the fifth lunar month. The local people rushed in boats to rescue or search for him. Some of them scattered Zongzi (glutinous rice dumplings wrapped in bamboo leaves) in the river, hoping to feed fish and shrimps lest they should eat away his body. An old doctor of traditional Chinese Medicine poured the realgar wine into the river to make river dragons drunk, otherwise they would hurt Qu Yuan. Later a river dragon came out of water with pieces of Qu Yuan's clothes. The people pulled the evil dragon onto the shore, cut its head off and took its

tendon out. It is said that the dragon's tendon could protect children from snakes or pests' attacks when it was bound around children's wrists or necks.

还有另外一个传说则说，屈原在五月初五投江之后，人们在每年的这一天都要把米装在竹筒里，投到江中祭祀他。有一次，有人梦见屈原。屈原说，多年来你们投的米都让蛟龙吃了。今年你们如果还要投的话，请在竹筒上面塞几张楝树叶子，再用五彩丝线绕在竹筒上，蛟龙见了害怕，就不会来抢了。后来，当地的人们就照着这个办法来祭奠屈原。据说用楝树叶和五彩丝线裹粽子，就是这样演变过来的。

Another legend says that after Qu Yuan drowned himself in the river on the fifth day of the fifth lunar month, people threw bamboo tubes with rice inside into the river on that day each year to offer sacrifices to him. One day someone had a dream that the rice thrown in the river had been eaten by river dragons. Qu Yuan told him in the dream that if they were to throw rice again this year, the bamboo tubes should be sealed with bamboo leaves and tied with five-colored threads, which would frighten river dragons away from the rice. Later the local people sacrificed for him in this way, from which rice, wrapped in bamboo leaves and five-colored threads, came to be known as Zongzi.

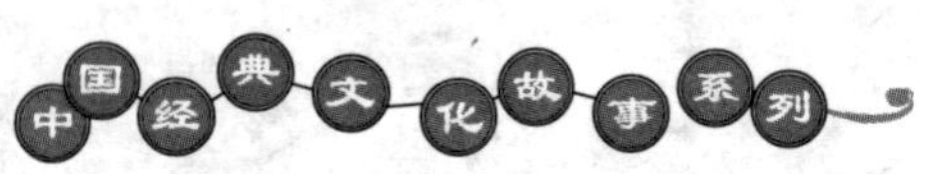

不难看出，这两个传说虽然都以屈原投江为核心，但具体说法却并不太一致。传说提到了端午节的一些风俗活动内容，诸如划龙舟、裹粽子、拴五色丝线、喝雄黄酒等，把它们一概说成是为了纪念屈原，可能也有些附会。不过许多人又都认为这样的传说寄托了民众对伟大爱国主义诗人屈原的追慕和崇敬，表达了民众的美好情感，还是应该珍惜的。屈原的诗歌代表作《离骚》、《九歌》、《天问》等，一向脍炙人口，光照文坛，屈原在诗歌创作上的伟大成就流传千古，以至于有人主张称端午节为“诗人节”。从这一点上说，人们对这方面的传说格外偏爱，也是在情理之中的。

It is clear that both legends are based on Qu Yuan's drowning in the river, but they are somewhat diverse in specific descriptions. The legends involved the activities in the Double-Fifth Festival such as dragon-boat racing, Zongzi-wrapping, five-colored-thread binding, and realgar-wine drinking. But it is farfetched that everything was exclusively done for commemorating Qu Yuan. However, many people believe that these legends express people's respect and reverence for Qu Yuan, the great patriotic poet. His masterpieces are classics in Chinese literature like *Lisao*, *Jiuge* and *Tianwen*. His achievements in poetic writing are so great that it is claimed that the Double-Fifth Festival should be called the Poets' Festival. So it is reasonable that people have preference for the legends.

然而，讨论节日的起源毕竟是一种科学，我们也不能凭感情用事。学者们在这方面的讨论一向十分热闹，归纳起来，大致有以下几种说法，是可以供我们参考的。一说，这是古代江南持龙图腾崇拜民族的祭祖活动纪念日；二说，它起源于三代的兰浴，周代就有朱索桃印饰门、艾人悬户、系五彩缕、持赤灵符等风俗，这些古俗中的巫术行为，都是为了禳灾避邪，而今天端午节的一些做法，正是周代古俗的遗存；三说，春秋战国时，越王勾践在此日操练水军，相沿成俗；四说，纪念介子推；五说，纪念屈原；六说，纪念伍子胥；七说，纪念曹娥；八说，祭“地腊”；九说，古人将五月初五视作“恶日”，忌讳在此日生子，因此便有了种种禳灾避邪的巫术行为；十说，“夏至”说，说如今端午节吃粽子、竞渡等活动内容，在南北朝的典籍里明明是记录为夏至日的事情，后来不知为什么就移到端午日去了。

However, the discussion of the origin of a festival should be scientific rather than emotional. There have been heated discussions among scholars, which can be summed up as follows. One theory is that the Double-Fifth Festival is the day on which the ethnic groups that worship dragon as a totem offered sacrifices to their ancestors. Another theory originated from the fragrant thoroughwort bath in the three dynasties of Xia (2070 BC — 1600 BC), Shang (1600 BC — 1046 BC) and Zhou (1046 BC—221 BC). In the Zhou Dynasty, people had the custom of decorating the doors with five-colored threads and buttons made of peach wood, hanging wormwood, binding the five-colored threads, and holding the magic figures to bring in good fortune, hoping to eliminate disasters and ward off evil spirits. Traces of the Zhou Dynasty's custom are easily found in today's celebrations. The third theory is that the Double-Fifth Festival is the day on which Gou Jian, the king of the State of Yue, drilled his marine troops during the Warring States Period (475 BC — 221 BC), which developed into the present custom. The fourth theory is about the commemoration of Jie Zitui. The fifth is about the commemoration of Qu Yuan. The sixth is about the commemoration of Wu Zixu. The seventh is about Cao Eh. The eighth is about the sacrifice for "Dila". The ninth is that the ancient Chinese considered the fifth day of the fifth lunar month as an evil day, and it was a taboo to deliver a baby on that day, which evolved into the sorcery of eliminating disasters and warding off evil spirits. The tenth is about the Summer Solstice. The customs of eating Zongzi, dragon-boat racing, etc. were all activities for the Summer Solstice recorded in the classic books in the Northern and Southern Dynasties (420 BC — 581 AD). But no one knows why they were adopted as the activities of the Double-Fifth Festival.

这样的讨论自然还可继续下去，我们不可能一下子就做出十分精确的结论。不过至少我们已经可以有这样一种印象：端午节风俗的形成，有一个历史积淀的过程，并非一蹴而就。一般认为，端午节正值季节转换，虫毒蠢动，疫病滋生，我们的祖先试图用种种巫术行为去禳解它，辟邪逐疫，以祈求人们在这一年里能够平安。这大概是后世端午节许多风俗习惯的原始意义吧。

Similar discussions are naturally continuous, so we cannot come to a definite conclusion at once. But we have at least the impression that the formation of the Double-Fifth Festival's customs is a historic accumulation, not accomplished overnight. It is generally believed that the Double-Fifth Festival is high time for the change of the seasons, in which insects are crawling and diseases are spreading rampantly. So our ancestors attempted to drive away evils and dispel diseases, pleading to be safe and sound in the coming year, which is the original intention of the later custom of the Double-Fifth Festival.

端午节的风俗活动，花样特别多，在不同的时空里，又会有所嬗变，大致归纳起来，主要有龙舟竞渡、吃粽子、插艾蒿、喝雄黄酒、拴五色丝线、佩戴香袋、悬挂钟馗像等。

The Double-Fifth Festival has a great variety of activities, which have evolved through different times and in different places, mainly involving dragon-boat racing, eating Zongzi, hanging wormwood, drinking realgar wine, binding five-colored thread, wearing a scent bag, hanging a portrait of

Zhong Kui, etc.

龙舟竞渡，历来是深受各地民众喜爱的节日活动。据闻一多考证，四千五百多年前的江南吴越水乡，就已经有了这种风俗。古代文献中所记叙的龙舟竞渡，往往还伴随着祭祀与巫术。时至今日，我们所见到的就已经是一项完全有益于身心健康的文娱体育活动了。从中传达出来的万众一心、奋斗拼搏的精神和昂扬向上的朝气，感染着每一个人，激励着每一个人。正因为如此，世界上凡是华人聚居的地方，往往便会有龙舟竞渡的精彩表演。1980 年起，赛龙舟已经被列入我国的体育比赛项目，每年都要举行“屈原杯”龙舟赛。端午风俗的魅力，由此可见一斑。

The Dragon-boat race is always a popular festival event in all parts of China. According to Wen Yiduo’s survey, it came into existence in the Wu Yue water-bound towns in the south of China more than 4,500 years ago. The description of a dragon-boat race in ancient literature was associated with sacrifice and witchcraft. Up till now, what we can see is a complete recreational event beneficial to the health of the body and the mind. The spirit of being united as one and exerting all one’s strength and the enthusiasm with high morale affects and inspires everyone. It is due to this that where there are Chinese, there are wonderful performances of dragon-boat races. From the 1980s on, the dragon-boat race is on the list of China’s sports competition events. Qu Yuan Cup Dragon-

Boat Race is held every year to present its charm.

粽子，是端午节的节令食品。不过如今它已不仅限于在端午节食用，它甚至漂洋过海到了世界上的许多国家，成为有着浓郁乡土情趣的中餐美食。据说，早在春秋时代，便已有筒粽和角黍，前者是把米放在竹筒里密封烤熟，后者是用茭白叶包黍米成牛角状煮熟。以后历代演变，便有了许许多多的样式。据说清代乾隆帝吃了“九子粽”，赞不绝口，还为它赋过诗呢。把九只大小不一样的粽子串在一起，用九种颜色的丝线扎成，就成了馈赠亲友的一份好礼。旧时民间往往用来象征早生贵子、多子多福。除此之外，裹粽子用的米和里边的馅心，各地也往往不尽相同，北京的小枣粽、山东的黄米粽、上海的猪油夹沙粽、嘉兴的鲜肉粽、陕西的蜂蜜凉粽、四川的椒盐粽……都是名声在外，值得一尝的。

Zongzi is the festival food traditionally served during the Double-Fifth Festival. Zongzi is not only food for the Double-Fifth Festival in China, but also has traveled over the seas and oceans to many countries in the world and becomes a delicious Chinese food with a strong Chinese flavor. It is said that as early as the Spring and Autumn Period (770 BC — 476 BC), Tongzong and Jiaoshu came into existence. The former was made of rice in the bamboo tubes and air-tightly baked while the latter was made of the broomcorn millet covered with wild rice leaves in cow-horn shapes and steamed. With the evolution over many dynasties, Zongzi is seen in various shapes with a variety of fillings. After eating it, Emperor Qianlong in Qing Dynasty (1644 AD — 1911 AD) spoke highly of the Jiuzi Zong and even wrote a poem about it. A cluster of nine Zongzi of different sizes on a string tied with nine-color threads was the right gift for relatives and friends, symbolizing that the earlier to have a son the better it was for a couple's life, and the more children the couple would have, the happier the couple would be. Besides, its rice and fillings are different in different places, for example, Beijing's Zongzi with fillings of little dates, Shangdong's with fillings of yellow rice, Shanghai's with fillings of lard and pasty red bean, Jiaxing's with fillings of fresh meat, Shanxi's cold Zongzi with fillings of honey and Sichuan's with fillings of pepper-salt. They are all well-known and tasty.

旧时的端午节，家家户户都会在门口挂艾草，插菖蒲。俗语说："蒲剑斩千妖，艾旗招百福。"有的地方还会在艾草下面挂一个大蒜头。还有的地方，在艾草、菖蒲、大蒜之外，再加榴花、龙船花，俗称"天中五端"。总之，当年这样做，都是有些巫术意味的，人们以为这些玩意儿可以袪鬼袪邪。不过也有人指出，其实艾和菖蒲一类植物中大多含有芳香油，可以杀虫防病。端午时节，天气转热，容易引发多种疾病，家家户户挂艾草，插菖蒲，还是有些实际功用的。有的人家在这一天还要用苍术、白芷来烟熏内室，它的效用也就更加显而易见了。

Families hung wormwood and calamus on the door for the traditional Double-Fifth Festival in ancient times. There is an old saying that calamus could chop monsters like a sword and wormwood could bring about blessings like a flag. Under the wormwood hangs a head of garlic in some places. Besides wormwood, calamus and garlic, there are pomegranate flowers and Morningstar lilies. They are known as the five plants in the world. In short, all the activities in the past involved witchcraft to dispel ghosts and evils. However, it has been pointed out that wormwood and calamus contain volatile oil, which can be used to kill insects and avoid diseases. Around the Double-Fifth Festival, with the weather turning warmer, people are more likely to be infected with diseases, so it is somewhat practical to hang wormwood and calamus on the door. Some families even use herbs like atractylodes roots and angelica roots to smoke their room to good effect.

如果进一步引申，人们在这一天喝雄黄酒，拴五色丝线，佩戴香袋，说到底也是这么回事。民间传说《白蛇传》就提到，白娘娘是在端午节这天，一时大意，喝了雄黄酒，才不得不显露了原形的。人们历来以为，雄黄酒可以祛邪。医生却告诉我们，雄黄酒有毒，最好不要饮用。不过拿来外用，却有消毒的功效。

So it is easy to see that drinking realgar wine, binding five-colored thread, and wearing scent bags are just for the same reason. It is mentioned in the folktale, *The Story of the White Snake*, that the white snake was so negligent in drinking realgar wine that her original form was revealed. People always believe that realgar wine can drive away evils, but doctors say that it is poisonous and undrinkable. If applied externally, it has the effect of disinfection.

正因为历来都以为端午节是“恶日”，这一天会有许多邪恶和晦气袭来，人们为了对付它们，便要动用巫术。用今天的话来说，也就是实施某种象征性的祛祟行为。比如有的地方用大红纸剪蜈蚣、蝎子、壁虎、蜘蛛、毒蛇的形状，称为“五毒”，贴在室内，表示镇压。给小孩子戴虎头帽，穿五毒衣、五毒裤，佩戴香袋，拴五色丝线，都是为了祛祟。有的地方还要在端午节吃“五黄”，指的是雄黄酒、黄鳝、黄鱼、黄瓜、咸鸭蛋，据说也是如此。

The Double-Fifth Festival is always regarded as an evil day on which evils and bad luck abound, so people have to use witchcraft to deal with them. In today’s wording, it is a kind of symbolic practice to drive away evils. For example, in some places, the red paper-cuts are posted indoors for the repression of the evils in the shape of a centipede, a scorpion, a house lizard, a spider and a poisonous snake called five poisons. To dress a child in a tiger-like cap, a coat and trousers with the patterns of the five poisons and a five-color thread is also to drive away evils. In some places people eat Five

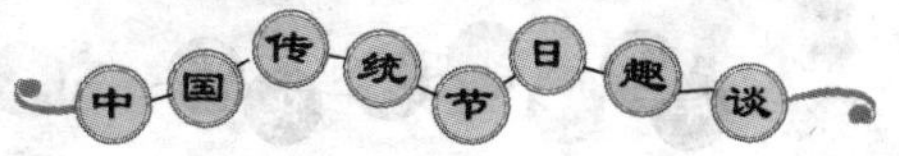

Yellows, like realgar wine, finless eel, yellow croaker, cucumber and salted duck eggs for the same reason.

悬挂钟馗像的目的，就更加直露。古人以为钟馗是捉鬼的能人，在家里挂上他的像，妖魔鬼怪就不敢进来了。传说钟馗是个进士，有一年考中状元。皇帝嫌他长得太丑，要把他赶出金銮殿。钟馗暴跳如雷，当场自杀，死后就成了捉鬼的神灵。奈何桥的守桥小鬼又化作蝙蝠，为他做向导。又说，钟馗死后，他的同乡好友杜平为他安葬。钟馗为了感恩，把妹妹嫁给了杜平。当年有一幅《钟馗嫁妹》图，在民间是十分流行的。

It is much easier to find out the purpose of hanging a portrait of Zhong Kui. The ancient Chinese thought that Zhong Kui was capable of eliminating ghosts and demons, and hanging his portrait up in their homes could keep off evil spirits. According to a legend, Zhong Kui took the examinations required to enter government services and got number one in the exams. But the Emperor thought he was so ugly that he was driven out of the imperial palace. Furious, Zhong Kui killed himself and became the spirit of catching ghosts. The ghost who was changed from a bat and guarded the Naihe Bridge worked for him as a guide. Another saying is that his town fellow, Du Ping buried him after his death. Zhong Kui married off his little sister to Du Ping in return. The picture of *Zhong Kui Marrying off his Sister* was very

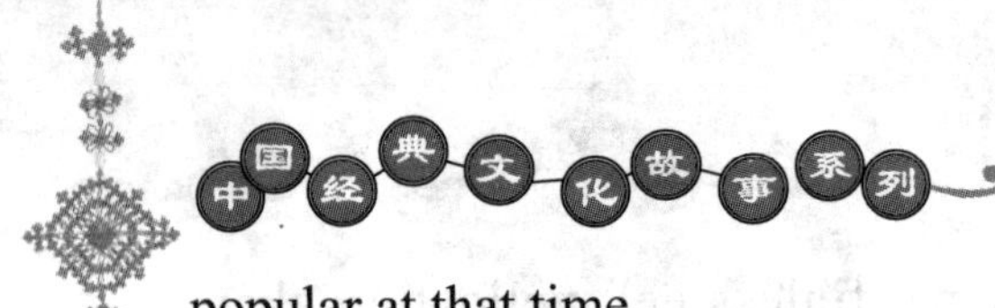

popular at that time.

不过有学者却指出，钟馗是虚构出来的。古代有终葵，也就是用来打击妖魔鬼怪的大木棒。后人以讹传讹，把终葵衍变成了钟馗，前后的读音则是一样的。作为一种节日风俗，钟馗捉鬼给人们留下了很深印象。钟馗的画和有关钟馗的传说故事、戏曲小说，更加异彩纷呈、引人入胜。这样一个貌丑而心美，对鬼凶而对人善的艺术形象，则是很值得我们珍惜的。

However, some scholars have pointed out that Zhong Kui is a fictional image. In ancient times there was a big stick called Zhong Kui which was used to fight against evils and demons. With the descendants passing on the message incorrectly, the two Chinese characters changed but the pronunciation remains the same. The festival custom that Zhong Kui catches ghosts is impressive. The pictures, legends, traditional operas, and novels relating to Zhong Kui are various and appealing. The artistic image of his ugliness in appearance but beauty in heart, his ferocity to ghosts but kindness to man is very valuable to us.

七、七夕节

7. The Double-Seventh Festival

农历七月初七，是中国传统节日中最具浪漫色彩的一个节日，俗称“七夕节”、“乞巧节”、“女儿节”。

The seventh day of the seventh lunar month is the most romantic traditional Chinese festival, commonly known as the Double-Seventh Festival, the Begging Festival or the Daughter's Festival.

为什么人们会对这个节日产生如此浓郁的兴趣呢？话还得从遥远的星空说起。

Why do people hold such a great interest in this festival? The story begins with the remote starry sky.

七夕，正是夏日，夜晚凉风轻拂，星光闪烁，人们抬头便看到星空里有一条横贯南北的天河。在天河东边，你可以找到一颗织女星，在一颗大星边上有四颗小星，看上去就像一只织布机。天河西边还有牵牛星，跟它遥遥相望，一大二小，看上去就像一副扁担。老人说，那就是牛郎挑着扁担，一前一后装着他的两个孩子，正急匆匆地去追赶他心爱的妻子织女，却被狠心的王母娘娘用一条天河把他们给隔开了。七夕的夜晚有这么一则凄哀动人的爱情故事相伴，怎不令人怦然心动！

On the night of the seventh day of the seventh lunar month, with cool summer breeze caressing the face and stars twinkling overhead, you may gaze up to where the Milky Way, or Heavenly River in Chinese, traverses the night sky from south to north. On the east bank, you will spot Vega, also called the Weaving Maid or Zhi Nu, with four small stars around; this constellation looks like a loom. Opposite to her, on the distant western bank, is Altair, one big star and two small ones, which looks like a shoulder pole. The elderly says that it is Cowherd or Niu Lang, who carries the shoulder pole with his two children on each end chasing his beloved wife Zhi Nu, but is separated by the cruel empress of Heaven with the Heavenly River. With such a tragic but beautiful story lingering in your mind on the Double-Seventh's Day, how can you suppress your upsurge of emotion?

和许多有关节日的传说一样，这则脍炙人口的《牛郎织女》也并非一蹴而就的。这中间有着一个萌生、孕育、发展、成熟的过程。据学者考证，早在春秋时代，《诗经》里就已经有歌咏“牵牛”与“织女”这两颗星的诗歌了。那时候的人很喜欢观看天上的星辰，他们发现了天河两边的这两颗星，分别给取了拟人化的名字，并且已经朦朦胧胧地要想为他们之间的某种情感编织故事了。这在《古诗十七首》中又一次可以找到证据，其中有

一首是这样唱的："迢迢牵牛星，皎皎河汉女；纤纤擢素手，札札弄机杼；终日不成章，泣涕零如雨。河汉清且浅，相去复几许，盈盈一水间，脉脉不得语。"他们为什么被隔开，具体细节似乎还不清楚。不过这种恋人间的相思情却已经深深地打动了每一位读者。

Just like many other legends related to festivals, this popular story of *Niu Lang and Zhi Nu* is not accomplished overnight. It has undergone the process of embryo, breeding, growth and maturity. According to scholars, early in the Spring and Autumn Period (770 BC — 476 BC) in Chinese history, there were poems about the two stars Niu Lang and Zhi Nu, collected in *Shi Jing* (*The Book of Songs*). People at that time liked to observe the stars; they detected these two stars across the Heavenly River, gave them personified names and subconsciously began to make up stories of their romance. Such evidence can be found in *Gu Shi Shiqishou* (*The Seventeen Ancient Poems*). It is described in one poem as follows:

Eagerly pining the Cowherd,
Brightly shining the Weaving Maid.
Fine fingers working on the loom,
All heard is lonely sound.
Within one day no bolts made,
Only sorrowful tears are shed.

Clear and deep the Heavenly River,
On earth where does it lead?
Affection carried and filled,
Whispers of love cannot be heard.

Specific explanations as for why they are separated remain unknown but their interwoven love has stirred the heart of every reader.

在汉代应劭的《风俗通义》里，我们可以读到织女七夕渡河，喜鹊为她搭桥的情节。在晋代葛洪的《西京杂记》里，又记下了汉代有七夕彩女穿七孔针于开襟楼的习俗。一直到南朝梁任昉的《述异记》，我们终于读到作者记下来的牛郎织女传说的完整情节。当然，与后世人们所讲述的故事相比，那段文字还是显得有些简略粗糙。

We may come across the story of the Weaving Maid crossing the Heavenly River on the Double-Seventh Festival with the help of magpies to form a bridge with their wings so that Zhi Nu might cross and meet her husband in *Fengsu Tongyi* (*Annotation of Literature and Customs*) by Ying Shao of the Han Dynasty (206 BC—220 AD). We may get to know the convention of weaving maids threading seven-holed needles at the Kaijin Building in the Han Dynasty in *Xijing Zaji* (*Miscellaneous Records of the Western Capital*) by Ge Hong of the Jin Dynasty (265 AD—420 AD). And eventually we may get the whole tale of Niu Lang and Zhi Nu in *Shuyi Ji* (*Record of Marvels*) by Liang Renfang of the South Dynasty (420 AD — 589 AD). Of course, the account is by no means delicate, to compare with the stories told by people afterwards.

在底层民众中，这则口头故事世代相传，不断被加工润色，时至今日，它的情节已经发展得相当感人了。

The folktale is passed from generation to generation, polished and enriched among the lower populace; so far, its plot has been fully developed and heart-touching.

都说牛郎是个苦命的孩子，父母早逝，哥嫂又虐待他，只有一头牛与他相依为命。一天，老牛给他出了个主意，说是天上的仙女要下凡来洗澡，你去偷走她们中间一个女子的衣裳，就可以娶她为妻了。到时候，天上果然飞下七只鸽子，一眨眼工夫变成七个漂亮的女子，在一个水池里洗澡。牛郎把其中最小的一个女子的衣服给藏了起来。另外六个女子变成鸽子飞回天上。最小的女子是织女，她没法飞走，就跟牛郎做了夫妻。

It is said that Niu Lang was a poor orphan, parents dead long ago, ill-treated by his elder brother and sister-in-law, with the only company of an old ox. One day, the old ox worked out a good idea for Niu Lang. He told Niu Lang that some fairies would descend to the earth to have a bath and Niu Lang would marry one of them if he could steal her dress. As predicted by the old ox, seven pigeons descended from the heaven, turned into seven beautiful fairies and came to bathe in a brook. Niu Lang concealed the youngest fairy's dress as told. The other six fairies turned into pigeons after the bath and ascended to the heaven, leaving the youngest, Zhi Nu, on the earth. Unable to join her sisters without her dress, Zhi Nu married Niu Lang.

牛郎织女相亲相爱，男耕女织，又生下了一儿一女，小日子过得蛮好。后来老牛要死了，叮嘱牛郎，把它的皮留着，遇到急难只要披上牛皮，就有办法解救。老牛死后，牛郎忍痛剥下牛皮，把老牛埋在山坡。

Mutually in love, Niu Lang worked on the farm, Zhi Nu wove cloth, and later they had a son and a daughter. Theirs was a happy family. Before passing away, the old ox exhorted Niu Lang to keep its hide after his death so that it would be helpful at crucial moments so long as Niu Lang put it on. After the death of the old ox, with a heavy heart, Niu Lang peeled off the ox's hide and buried the ox at a hillside.

天上的王母娘娘终于发觉织女私自下凡，勃然大怒，当即派天兵天将下凡，把织女抓了回去。牛郎那天正在耕地，回家一看，可不得了，马上披上牛皮，用扁担把两个孩子也挑上，急匆匆去追赶织女。牛皮有魔力，牛郎一下子就腾空飞了起

来，眼看要追上织女啦。

In the event, the Empress of Heaven got to know Zhi Nu's secret marriage to Niu Lang. Flying into a rage, she sent the heavenly soldiers to arrest Zhi Nu. Niu Lang was ploughing in the field that day when Zhi Nu was taken away. When he returned home, he was taken aback and put on the ox hide immediately with his two children carried by a shoulder pole. The magic of the ox hide enabled him to fly up and soon he was about to catch up with Zhi Nu.

王母娘娘急了，拔下头上的金簪一划，顿时在织女身后出现一条天河，浊浪滔滔，谁也过不去。牛郎被隔在天河的对岸，急得双脚跳，却毫无办法。牛郎的两个孩子有志气，就蹲在天河边上舀水，下决心要把天河水舀干，过河去见娘。

The Empress was quick enough to take off her gold hairpin to draw a line. At once, behind Zhi Nu emerged a heavenly river with roaring waves, too dangerous for anyone's attempt to cross. Separated on the opposite bank, Niu Lang could do nothing but stamp his feet with anxiety in vain. Niu Lang's two children were so ambitious that they squatted by the river starting to ladle the water, determined to ladle out the water to meet their mother.

王母娘娘也被牛郎织女一家人的真挚情感打动了，只好准许他们每年七月初七相会一次。这一天，人间的喜鹊全都会飞上天，互相咬着尾巴，在天河上搭桥。牛郎织女踩在一只只喜鹊的头上走过去聚会。你去看喜鹊的头顶总是光秃秃的，为啥？据说就是踩出来的。人们还说，这一天夜深人静的时候，如果躲在瓜果架下，兴许还能听到牛郎织女相互诉说的脉脉情话哩。

The family's true feelings moved the Empress too and she had to permit them to meet every seventh day of the seventh lunar month. On that day, all the magpies on the earth would fly up to the heaven, holding each other's tail in the mouth, to make a magpie bridge over the Heavenly River. Niu Lang and Zhi Nu would walk towards each other on the magpies' heads to meet. You may notice that the head tops of magpies are always bald. Why? It is said that is because of the trampling. People also say that in the still of that night, if you hide yourself under the fruit trellis, you might overhear the sweet conversations between Niu Lang and Zhi Nu.

鹊桥相会的故事自然是编出来的，不过它传达出来的人们对爱情生活和自由幸福的渴望，却是真实的，又是强烈的。千百年来，《牛郎织女》传说伴随着七夕节，走进千家万户，也被许多文人不断传诵，留下了无数优美篇章。

There is no doubt that their meeting on the magpie bridge is a made-up story but the conveyed message of people's desire for life of love and happiness of freedom is real and strong.

Over thousands of years, the tale of *Niu Lang and Zhi Nu*, together with the Double-Seventh Festival, has been familiar to a great number of families and inspired many men of letters to compose elegant proses.

七夕节的主要民俗活动是乞巧。妇女们在这天夜里总要聚在一起，十分认真地祭拜牛郎星和织女星。据说织女心灵手巧，是个纺织能手，所以妇女们总是要向她祈求，让自己也能心灵手巧，俗称“乞巧”。也有乞富、乞寿、乞子的，各人可以有所选择。不过俗信以为，不能兼求，只可求其一。说起来，传说中的织女是个苦命人，别无所长，只是心灵手巧而已，所以更多的人在这时候是乞巧。

Skills-begging is the main folk custom for the Double-Seventh Festival, on which night women would get together to pray to Vega and Altair. Zhi Nu is said to be clever and deft, good at handicraft, so women always pray to her for the special gift, which is called skills-begging. There are also those who pray for wealth, long life or sons, each having her own preferable choice, but only one wish can be prayed for according to the folk belief. As the folktale goes, Zhi Nu is a wretched maid, nothing but clever and deft; therefore more women tend to pray for her special gift.

祭祀牛郎织女的供品也别具一格，一般都用瓜、花、菱、藕、桃、李、莲蓬一类，显得清新纤巧，与通常由男子主持的那种祭祀仪式中所常见的大鱼大肉形成了鲜明的对比。

The sacrifice offered to Niu Lang and Zhi Nu are distinctive — melons, flowers, water chestnuts, peaches, plums, lotus seedpods, etc. —fresh and dainty, in remarkable contrast to the usual fish and meat offered at those common memorial ceremonies hosted by male masters.

乞巧的形式也有多种。较常见的是穿针。一群女孩子，手拿丝线，对着月光比赛穿针，看谁先穿过就是“得巧”，这是一种颇受人欢迎的闺中游戏。传说唐代有个郑采娘，在七夕夜祭拜织女，向织女祈求。织女问她，你求什么？她说我要乞巧。织女便送她一枚一寸多长的金针，插在一张纸上，又说三天之内不得告诉任何人，即可得巧，还可变为男子。两天后，她忍不住把这事说给母亲听，母亲去看金针，却没了踪影，只留下有着针迹的一张纸。而郑采娘死后，据说果然托生成了一个男孩。后世的女子纷纷仿效，穿针乞巧便蔚然成风。

Skills-begging takes varied forms; the common one is threading the needle. A group of unmarried girls, with threads in hand, perform a small contest of threading the needle in the moonlight and the one who first threads the needle will win the special gift from Zhi Nu. It is a very popular game among maids. There is a story about a maid named Zheng Cainiang who prayed to Vega on the night of the Double-

Seventh Festival. Zhi Nu asked her what she desired and she answered "weaving crafts". Zhi Nu then gave her a one-inch gold needle and stuck it in a piece of paper, saying that within three days without letting anybody know Zhen Cainiang would receive the special gift and could also change into a lad. Two days later, Zheng Cainiang could not help but reveal the secret to her mother who went to see the gold needle out of curiosity, only to find nothing but the paper with the needle hole in it. After her death, Zheng Cainiang was said to be reincarnated to a baby boy. Afterwards, maids followed suit and thus threading the needle to beg for the special gift has become a popular practice.

《开元天宝遗事》这本书记载了唐玄宗时候的不少掌故，其中则提到，当时的宫中流行另一种“乞巧”：七夕，人们都去捉来蜘蛛，放进一个小盒，第二天清晨打开小盒，比谁的蜘蛛结的网更密。密的为巧多，稀的为巧少。后来民间也竞相仿效，颇具情趣。

One of the anecdotes kept in the book *Kaiyuan Tianbao Yishi* [*Bequeathed Matters from the Kaiyuan* (713 AD — 741 AD) *and Tianbao* (742 AD — 756 AD) Periods], about the time of Emperor Tang Xuanzong of the Tang Dynasty (618 AD — 907 AD), mentions that there was another form of "skills-begging" in the palace at that time: On the night of the Double-Seventh Festival, the palace maids would each get a spider, put it into a small box, and open the box the next early morning to see whose spider had woven a thicker web; the thicker web showed the owner's being bestowed on more weaving skills, the thinner fewer. Accordingly, the folk populace contended to take the practice, which was of great appeal.

在江南一带，老人们回忆，她们小时候的“七夕乞巧”则又是一番风味。早在七夕前一天，人们就要取来雨水、井水各一半，盛在一只碗里，放在露天，承接一夜露水，再放在太阳底下晒半天，到了中午，水面便会生成薄薄的一层水膜。再将一枚绣花针，或一根极细的竹丝、松针，轻轻放入，让它浮在水膜之上而不下沉，再来看针在水底映出的影子。由于种种偶然因素，再加上人们的想象，那针影常会变幻无穷，如果像龙凤，像云彩，像花卉，就以为乞得了巧，预兆这个女孩将来一定心灵手巧，事事如意。这种活动往往是许多女孩聚在一起进行的，俗称“乞巧会”，欢声笑语，格外愉悦。

In the south area by the Changjiang River, according to the memories of the elderly women, the begging activity in their childhood had a different aspect of interest. Early on the day before the Double-Seventh Festival, people would fetch rainwater and well-water in equal quantity and put the mixed water in a bowl in the open air for a whole night. The next morning on the Double-Seventh Festival, the bowl of water which contained night dew too would be put under the sun for half a day till the noon when a thin film emerged on the surface of the water. Then an embroidery needle, or an extremely thin bamboo strand, or a pine needle would be put on the surface slightly enough that it would float but not sink. Judgment would be made according to the needle shadows reflected from the bottom of the water. Due to accidental factors, coupled with people's imagination, the needle shadows would change constantly and magically. It was taken for granted that the form of a dragon, a phoenix, or clouds or flowers was a sign of receiving the special gift, a prediction that the girl would be clever and deft and get whatever she aspired after. Such an activity was always performed when lots of girls gathered together, known as "the Begging Gathering", which was full of delightful laughter and cheerful exchanges of conversations.

在广州民间，女子们在七夕夜祭拜的同时，还会在供桌上展示各自的“女红”，诸如她们亲手做的绣花鞋、虎头帽、香荷包、剪纸窗花和各色手工艺，琳琅满目，美不胜收，让亲友和过往行人观赏评论。

Among the folk populace in Guangzhou, while worshipping on the night of the Double-Seventh Festival, girls will display their own needlework on the offering table, such as their hand-made embroidered shoes, tiger-head hats, scented purses, paper-cuts and many other articles of handicraft art, which is a feast for the eyes, too much to enjoy. Friends, relatives and passers-by cannot help stopping to appreciate and comment.

在一些地方，还有七夕看巧云的风俗。人们认为这一天的云彩特别会变幻，看云彩变幻成什么形状，来猜测自己的命运。这似乎有点玄，和前面说的看针影有相似之处，往往是心理作用在左右着人们。农村里的老人，据说还要在七夕夜看天河，说是倘若这一年天河出现得早，就预兆这一年丰收，米价贱；倘若出现迟，就预兆米价要上涨，俗称“探米价”。这是一种古老的占卜术，如今也已淡出了人们的记忆。

In some areas, there is a custom of gazing up at clouds on the Double-Seventh Festival. People presume that that day's clouds tend to take special magic changing forms and they like to conjecture about their fates in accordance with the changeable clouds. This seems somewhat mysterious as the above-mentioned needle shadows, under the influence exerted by people's psychology. The elderly in the countryside are said to observe the Heavenly River whose early appearance is said to predict a harvest year with a low corn price; otherwise, a high corn price. People call it "An Inquiry about

Corn Price", an old practice of divination, which so far has faded out of people's memory.

江南的村姑还有七夕洗头发的习俗。她们相约到野外采摘七种野草，揉出青汁，拿来洗头发。后来一般又都是采摘一种槿树叶，泡水洗头。传说织女总会在这一天到河边洗头发，把头发洗得乌黑锃亮，再去见牛郎。于是凡间的女子也都学她的样，要在这一天洗头。

The country girls in the south of the Changjiang River have the custom of washing hair on the Double-Seventh Festival. Originally, they went to the field to collect seven kinds of weeds from which they rubbed juice out for hair washing. Later, hair was washed with water mixed with hibiscus leaves to substitute for weeds. It is said that Zhi Nu will wash her hair by the riverside that day and go to meet Niu Lang when her hair takes a glossy black look. Thus girls on the earth wash their hair too on that day.

还有一种节日点心也必须提到。用面粉加些糖，糅合，压成薄片，切做小方块，稍加扭曲，放到油里去炸，就跟麻花似的，甜脆可口，不过更加小巧玲珑，又有着一个很好听的名字，叫"巧果"，似乎暗含着乞巧的意思在里头。许多人家都会自己做，也有的商店专门做这种生意，销路总是蛮好的。

We cannot miss mentioning one snack for the festival.

Dough is mixed with sugar, kneaded, pressed into a thin piece, cut into small squares, twisted slightly and put into boiled oil to fry. The snack tastes sweet and crisp, the shape of which resembles Mahua (a fried dough twist), but more dainty and has a nice name "Qiao Guo" with the implication of "skills-begging". It is usually home-made; some stores run this business as well and it sells well.

如今，七夕乞巧的风俗似乎正在淡化，不过牛郎织女的传统却依旧在人们的口耳间广为流传。有人说，外国有情人节，中国人也应该有自己的情人节。而在传统节日里边，把七夕节当做情人节来过，那倒是蛮合适的，你说呢？

Till now, the begging mores on the Double-Seventh Festival seem to fade out, but the legend of Niu Lang and Zhi Nu is still on the lips of people. Since Valentine's Day is celebrated in foreign countries, some say, the Chinese should observe their own Valentine's Day too. Among the traditional festivals, the Double-Seventh Festival is better suited to Valentine's Day. Won't you agree?

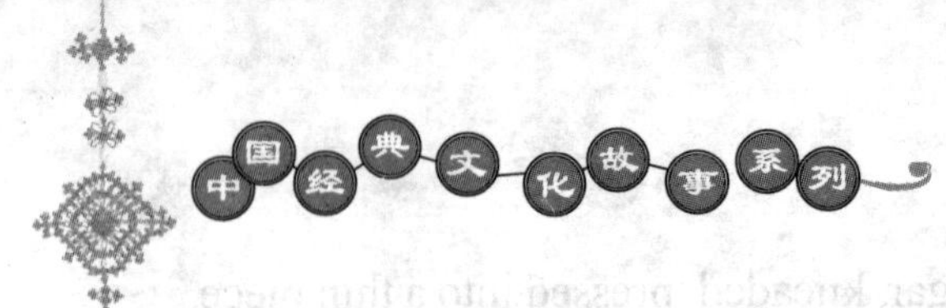

八、中元节

8. The Hungry-Ghost Festival

中元节在农历七月十五日，俗称“七月半”，又称“盂兰盆节”、“鬼节”。起源于宗教，后来走向民间，又成为传统的祭祖日。关于它的起源，一般有两种说法。

The Hungry-Ghost Festival falls on the 15th of the 7th lunar month, commonly known as “ the Mid-July”, or “Ullambana”, “the Ghost Festival”. It originated from religion, became popular among the populace and finally evolved into the traditional memorial day for ancestors. Generally speaking, there are two versions concerning its origin.

一说起源于道教。道教信仰三官神，指的是天官、地官、水官。不难看出，这是原始信仰里对于天、地、水的自然崇拜到了后世的一种衍变。后人将自然崇拜人格化，以为在冥冥之中有三个神在主管着天、地、水，如此而已。既然是人格神，当然得有他们的诞生日。大约在宋代，人们就约定俗成，以为天官的生日是正月十五，地官的生日是七月十五，水官的生日是十月十五。这三个日子分别称为上元、中元、下元，合称“三元”。道教以为，地官会在每年七月十五日这一天下降人间，判定人间善恶。旧时，大小道观都要在这一天作斋醮荐福。《梦粱录》称，

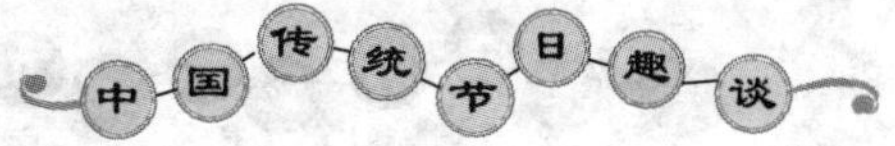

这一天为“解制日”。《道经》则说，这一天道观诵经，是为了使得“囚徒饿鬼，当时解脱”。南宋时的临安，每到这一天都要在钱塘江里放水灯万盏，场面颇为壮观。这里都有着超度和解脱的意图在里面。

One version said that it originated from Taoism, which worships three gods—God of Heaven, God of Earth and God of Water. Obviously, it is an evolution from the natural worship for heaven, earth and water at ancient times. Later, the natural worship was personified and it was presumed that there were three gods in charge of heaven, earth and water imperceptibly but inexorably. Since they were personified gods, they should have their birthdays. In the Song Dynasty (960 AD—1279 AD), it was accepted as a common practice that the birthday of God of Heaven fell on the 15th of the first lunar month , the birthday of God of Earth on the 15th of the seventh lunar month and the birthday of God of Water on the 15th of the tenth lunar month. These three dates were respectively called the First 15th, the Mid-15th and the Last 15th, collectively known as Three 15ths. According to Taoism, God of Earth would descend to the earth on the 15th of the seventh lunar month to give judgment upon men's deeds. In the old days, on that day, in Taoist temples, big or small, a ritual would be held to pray for blessings. The day is called "Exonerating Day" in *Meng Liang Lu* (*Record of the Golden Millet Dream*).

It is mentioned in *Taoist Scriptures* that prayers are said in temples on that day to "exonerate the hungry and imprisoned ghosts". In Lin'an City in the Southern Song Dynasty (1127 AD—1279 AD), people would float millions of lanterns along the Qiangtang River with the intention of releasing souls from the hell, which presented a splendid sight.

一说起源于佛教。佛教里有《盂兰盆经》，说的是一个颇为有名的"目连救母"的故事。这个故事传入中国后，又敷衍成变文，广为流传。宋代，有人将其搬上戏曲舞台，成为一个剧目。明清以降，又在民间逐渐形成了一种"目连戏"，专门搬演"目连救母"一类故事，俗称"鬼戏"。每到中元节，许多地方都会请戏班来演这种目连戏。目连救母的故事，大致是说目连的母亲生前做了许多恶事，死后被打入地狱吃苦。目连决心救母，遍历地狱，寻找母亲，最后终于将母亲救出。故事情节曲折离奇，极力铺叙地狱的恐怖，自然有其消极的一面。不过经过历代民间艺人的创造，戏里又常常会闪耀出人性的光彩，曲折地表达出底层民众的心声。鲁迅生先曾写过《无常》、《女吊》等文章，对于传统的目连戏艺术就有过极高的评价。

The other version said that it originated from Buddhism, whose *Ullambana Scriptures* records a very popular story "The Great Maudgalyayana Rescues His Mother from the Hell". When the story was delivered to China, it was translated into alternate prose and rhyming lines and spread widely. In the

Song Dynasty (960 AD — 1279 AD), it was staged and became a traditional play. During the Ming and Qing dynasties (1368 AD— 1911 AD), Maudgalyayana plays came into shape among the populace, which staged stories like "The Great Maudgalyayana Rescues His Mother from the Hell", commonly known as "ghost plays". In many places, theatrical companies would be invited to perform such plays on the Hungry-Ghost Festival. "The Great Maudgalyayana Rescues His Mother from the Hell" goes as follows: Maudgalyayana's mother conducted lots of vicious deeds while alive and was sent to Hell to suffer after her death; Maudgalyayana was determined to rescue her, traveling around the Hell in search of her, and finally got her out. The plot is complicated and bizarre, and the horror of the Hell is greatly exaggerated, the negative factors of which are obviously revealed. However, re-created by folk artists through many generations, splendor of humanity always stands out to indirectly reflect the lower populace's aspirations. Mr. Lu Xun gave high comment on the traditional Maudgalyayana plays in his essays such as *Wu Chang and Nu Diao*.

我们知道，中国民众对于宗教一向是兼收并蓄的，他们不大有什么门户之见，儒释道往往会纠缠不清，中元节就是一个例证。大约到了南北朝的时候，人们就会在这一天里同时请和尚道士一起来念经，主要是追荐自己的祖先亡灵。江南俗谚："七月十二接祖宗，西瓜老藕瞎莲蓬。"说的就是"中元接祖"习俗。旧时，家家户户都会在中元节祭祖。有的人家，要提前到七月十二日，就把祖先"接"过来了。新丧之家，还要请僧道到家中拜忏念经，格外隆重。俗信又以为，当年目连救母时打开了地狱的大门，许多孤魂野鬼趁机逃出了地狱，在世上到处流浪，他们很是可怜，弄不好还会惹是生非，所以也需要给他们一些施舍，以示安抚，或者说是为了帮助他们解脱苦难。而这样做其实也是为了自己的祖先，否则的话，孤魂野鬼捣乱，自己的祖先也就不得安宁了。

It is widely known that the Chinese people hold an all-embracing attitude towards religion and harbor no prejudice against different schools. Therefore, Confucianism, Buddhism and Taoism are always entangled, and the Hungry-Ghost Festival is a good illustration. During the period of the Northern and Southern Dynasties (429 AD—581 AD), people would invite both Buddhist monks and Taoists to say prayers to honor family ancestors. "On the 12th day of the seventh lunar month family ancestors are received, with watermelons, lotus roots and seedpods as offerings", an old saying prevailing to the south of the Changjiang River, refers to the custom of "ancestors-receiving" on the Hungry-Ghost Festival on the 15th of the seventh lunar month; some families even "received" their ancestors on the 12th in advance. Those who recently lost their family members would invite monks and Taoists home to say prayers to release souls from the Hell, the scene of which was indescribably grand. People commonly believed that since Maudgalyayana threw the gate of the Hell open when he rescued his mother, many lonely spirits seized the chance to escape from the Hell and wandered around the earth. These poor spirits would stir up trouble if offended, so alms should be offered to appease them or to relieve them from misery. But it was also for the benefit of the ancestors because if lonely spirits stirred up trouble the ancestors would not rest in peace.

当年，超度孤魂野鬼的一种重要风俗是“放河灯”，还有“放焰口”，据说都是作为对孤魂野鬼的超度和安抚。放河灯的风俗，如今在许多地方都保留了下来，把无数盏小灯放入江河之中，

通常都会做成荷花形状，任其漂流，据说是为了给黑暗中的亡灵带去一些光明。映衬着茫茫夜色，水面上浮动着成千上万盏酷似荷花的水灯，这种场面实在是很让人怦然心动的。把它看做一种传统的“行为艺术”，也未尝不可。在一些地方，这一天要祭扫祖坟，而在祭扫祖坟的同时，人们也总会在路边焚烧一些纸钱，据说那就是烧给孤魂野鬼的，称之为“祀孤魂”。在某种意义上说，这种尊祖尽孝的传统和普度众生的慈悲胸怀，同样是传统美德的一部分，也是值得我们珍惜的。所以在一些地方，又把这一天叫做“母亲节”，或是叫做“忏悔节”、“解脱节”，其中的意蕴很值得我们细细体味。

“Floating lanterns” and “setting off fireworks” used to be the main custom to pacify the wandering spirits. Now, “floating lanterns” is still practiced in many places. People float myriads of lanterns in the shape of the lotus on the river, which is meant to bring some bright light to those souls in the dark. With the dim light of the vast night at the background, millions of lanterns resembling lotuses are drifting on the river and your heart cannot but be stirred with excitement and amazement. It would not be wrong to say that it is a kind of traditional art of behavior. On the Hungry-Ghost Festival, people will offer sacrifices to their ancestors in front of the ancestor graves, and meanwhile burn some spirit money by the road for those lonely souls, known as “sacrifices to lonely souls”. In some sense, the customs of paying reverence and devotion to ancestors and the broad-mindedness of delivering the multitude of people from misery belong to part of traditional virtues, which deserve our observation. So in some places, people also name the day “Mother’s Day”, “Repenting Day” or “Exonerating Day”, the meaning of which is profound and calls for our careful consideration.

九、中秋节

9. The Mid-Autumn Festival

月到中秋分外明。

The harvest moon is exceptionally bright.

中秋节在夏历八月十五日，又称“仲秋节”、“团圆节”。都说这一天夜里的月亮最圆最亮。这时候秋高气爽，正适宜赏月，合家团聚赏月便成为这个节日的主要特征。为什么叫“中秋”呢？农历七、八、九月为秋季，八月居中，为“中秋”。又说，每季之月依次为孟、仲、季，八月为仲秋，“仲”通“中”，故名“中秋”。

The Mid-Autumn Festival, also known as the Zhongqiu Festival, or the Reunion Festival, falls on the fifteenth day of the eighth lunar month when the moon is at its fullest and brightest at night. Families usually celebrate this festival by gathering together, eating moon-cakes (round-shaped to symbolize perfection and union) and watching the bright moon. Why is it called Mid-Autumn? According to the Chinese lunar calendar, the seventh, eighth and ninth months are all in the season of autumn with the eighth lunar month in the middle. And the sequence of months in any season is listed

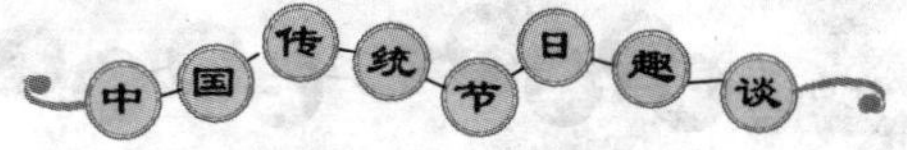

as *meng* (first), *zhong* (second) and *ji* (third) in Chinese. The Chinese character *zhong* (second) is homonymous with the character *zhong* (middle). The festival has got the name the Mid-Autumn Festival because it is in the middle of the autumn season.

中秋节由来已久，如果从人们对月亮的崇拜说起，那就更加悠远了。至少在《周礼》中就已提到“中秋夜迎寒”，估计那是周天子在这一天夜里祭月的一种仪礼吧。然而《荆楚岁时记》却并没提到中秋，可能南北朝时此俗尚未定型。不过到了唐代，中秋节已经颇有些名声，那是毫无疑问的。有好几种古籍都记述了风流天子唐明皇在这天夜里游月宫的生动传说，可见当时的中秋节已经成为一个很热闹的节日，才会催生出如此浪漫的篇章。

The Mid-Autumn Festival is of long standing and can be traced back to the worship of the moon in ancient times. The word Mid-Autumn was mentioned in the ancient book *Zhou Li* (*The Rites of Zhou*), which was estimated to refer to a sacrificial rite held by the emperor of the Zhou Dynasty (1046 BC —221 BC). But the custom did not take shape till the Northern and Southern dynasties (420 AD—581 AD), as it was not mentioned in the book of *Jingchu Suishiji* (*Festivals in the Jingchu Area*). It is certain that the Mid-Autumn Festival was popular in the Tang Dynasty (618 AD—907 AD) because according to some books, legend had it that Emperor Ming of

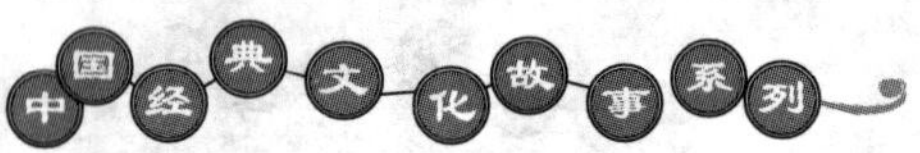

the Tang Dynasty traveled to the Moon Palace that night, showing that the Mid-Autumn Festival had become a lively festival from which the romance arose.

有关中秋的传说很多，嫦娥奔月、吴刚伐桂、玉兔捣药、唐明皇游月宫、八月十五天门开、月饼的来历……一个比一个生动，一个比一个精彩。在皎洁的月光下，听妈妈讲述这些动听的故事，是孩子们最好的享受。

The Mid-Autumn Festival involves many vivid and wonderful legends, such as Chang'e's Flight to the Moon, Wu Gang Chopping Down a Cassia Tree, The Jade Rabbit Pounding Medicine, Emperor Ming of the Tang Dynasty Traveling to the Moon Palace, the Opening of the Door to Heaven on the Fifteenth Day of the Eighth Month and The Origin of the Moon-Cakes. It is an enjoyable time for the Chinese children to listen to such amusing stories told by their mothers in the bright moonlight.

嫦娥是后羿的妻子。据说在很早很早的时候天上出现了十个太阳，给神州大地带来可怕的灾难，到处燃起熊熊烈火，河流干涸，横尸遍野。为了替天下的百姓除害，后羿一口气射下九个太阳。后来，他又继续拼搏，杀死了许多毒蛇猛兽，人们才终于能够安居乐业。不过世界上的事情往往不可能十全十美，后羿这样一个盖世英雄却也有他的不幸。他一天到晚在外面奔波，就冷落了他那美丽的妻子嫦娥。他们夫妻之间的感情终于出现了危机。据说后羿从西王母那儿要来了一包“不死之药”，一直是交给嫦娥珍藏的。那天，嫦娥一时想不开，偷吃了这药，就独自一个人升上云天，来到了寒冷的月宫。后羿知道了这事，想去追赶妻子，早已经来不及了。他原本是可以用弓箭去射月亮的，不过他毕竟于心不忍，最终还是没有射。嫦娥独自一人住在月宫里，只有一只玉兔和一只蟾蜍陪伴着她。玉兔整天在捣药，很是凄凉。李商隐的诗句：“嫦娥应悔偷灵药，碧海青天夜夜心。”说的就是这种心情。民间口耳相传，关于嫦娥奔月的传说后来又出现了许多不同的“版本”，众说纷纭，要为嫦娥奔月寻找另外一些理由。毕竟月亮是美的，嫦娥也是美的，人们希望嫦娥奔月的传说更加美一些，这种心情完全可以理解。

Chang’e was Houyi’s wife. A legend has it that long long ago, there were ten suns in the sky which brought about dreadful calamities to the earth with flames raging, the rivers getting dry and the corpses piling up. Houyi shot down nine suns with arrows in one breath, hoping to get rid of the evils for the people. Later he continued to kill the serpents and wild animals. As a result, people lived and worked peacefully and comfortably. But nothing can be perfect. Houyi, an unparalleled hero, was no exception, who experienced his misfortunes. He was out all day and gave his beautiful wife, Chang’e, the cold shoulder, which affected their mutual attachment. It was said that Houyi had asked for a packet of

pills, the elixir of life, from the Queen Mother and asked Chang'e to keep it. One day, Chang'e was so pessimistic that she ascended to the sky and arrived at the cold Moon Palace after swallowing the pills. When Houyi got to know this, it was too late for him to catch up with his wife. He could have shot at the moon with his arrow, but he did not have the heart to do so and gave up at last. Chang'e stayed alone in the Moon Palace with the Jade Rabbit and a toad as her company. The Jade Rabbit lived a dreary life, pounding medicine all day. The life there was described in Li Shangyin's poem, "Chang'e must regret stealing the elixir / As she broods in loneliness night after night". There are many variations of Chang'e legend as to the reason why she flew to the moon. It is understandable that all the legends are involved with the beauty of both the moon and Chang'e and they are the reflections of people's expectations.

吴刚伐桂的说法也有多种。古书上说，吴刚学仙，犯了错误，天帝罚他在月宫里砍伐一棵桂树。什么时候砍断了，他就算是解脱了。可是这棵桂树很怪，吴刚的斧子砍下去，树上有了一个缺口；可是等他把斧子再次挥起，那个缺口便又弥合了。于是吴刚只好一辈子在月宫里伐桂。

There are also various versions of Wu Gang's chopping down a cassia tree. According to one book, Wu Gang made a mistake while learning to be a celestial being. As a result, he got the punishment of chopping a cassia tree in the Moon Palace from the Jade Emperor of Heaven. He could not be freed from the punishment until he finally cut down the tree. But whenever he chopped, wounds of the tree would heal simultaneously, so he had to devote all his life to chopping in the Moon Palace.

有一年中秋节，唐明皇在宫里赏月。边上的道士罗公远一时高兴，要陪唐明皇到月宫里去玩玩。他随手把拐杖抛向空中，便成了一座天桥，两人踏着天桥上天，进了月宫。这时候，仙女们正在跳着《霓裳羽衣曲》，舞姿优雅，飘逸飞扬，美极啦。唐明皇是个绝顶聪明的人，在边上听了一遍，居然就把这个曲子给记了下来。据说如今我们听到的这个曲子，就是当年唐明皇从月宫里带回来的。

On one Mid-Autumn Festival, Emperor Ming of the Tang Dynasty enjoyed the moon in his palace together with Luo Gong, a Taoist priest, who, out of delight, suggested going on a pleasure journey with the emperor to the Moon Palace. He tossed his walking-stick into the air which turned into a bridge leading to the sky. The two of them walked over the bridge and came to the Moon Palace where the fairy maidens were dancing gracefully to the music of *The Dance in Leathery Clothes*. The emperor was so intelligent that he wrote down the tune after listening to it only once. It is said that the tune to which we listen today is the one he brought back from the Moon Palace.

又说“八月十五天门开”，中秋节夜里，月宫里的桂花树会降落桂子，如果地上的凡人拣到了，便会获得幸福。就在杭州西湖灵隐寺的边上，有一座山峰叫做月桂峰，据说便与这个掌故有关。

The story of “Opening the Door to Heaven on the Fifteenth of the Eighth Lunar Month” goes like this: The fruits of cassia trees fell down in the Moon Palace. The ordinary people who picked them up would gain happiness. The Cassia Peak, on the side of the Lingyin Temple near the West Lake in Hangzhou, is relevant to this legend.

中秋节吃月饼。关于月饼的传说也有好几种。有人说，这要追溯到当年七仙女和董永的爱情故事。七仙女回天宫，给董永留下一个儿子。儿子长大了，哭着找娘。吴刚听见了，不忍心，扮成村夫模样来见这个孩子，送给他一双登云鞋，让他中秋节穿了去见娘。那天，孩子上天，果然见到了娘。七仙女给儿子做饼吃，这饼就跟月亮似的，滚圆滚圆。后来，天帝发觉了这事，把吴刚罚到月宫里去伐桂，又把七仙女儿子的登云鞋没收了，遣送下凡。这孩子回到人间，思念亲娘，就做娘给他吃的那种饼，在中秋节那天把饼摆在月亮底下，表示对亲人的思念。据说这就是后来的月饼。

There are several legends about the custom of eating moon-cakes on the Mid-Autumn Festival. This custom can be traced back to the love story between Dong Yong and the Seventh Fairy Lady, who returned to the Palace in the sky leaving a son to Dong Yong. The son grew up and cried for his mother, so Wu Gang had to disguise himself as a farmer and gave his son a pair of shoes which could take him to see his mother in the Palace on the Mid-Autumn Festival. The son saw his mother and ate the cakes his mother made, which were round as the moon. Having been noticed by the Emperor of Heaven, Wu Gang was punished by chopping a cassia tree in the Moon Palace, and the son was sent back to the earth and the shoes were taken back. After coming back to the earth, the son missed his mother so much that he made the same cakes. Displayed in the moonlight on the night of the Mid-Autumn Festival, the cakes, symbolizing the longing for the relatives, are the moon-cakes today.

还有一种说法，说是为了反抗元朝统治，有人在中秋节前暗中串联，把“八月十五，家家齐动手”的纸条藏在饼里互相传递，作为一种联络暗号。中秋夜，家家户户吃了这饼，齐心协力起来造反，终于获得成功。从此以后，中秋吃月饼也就蔚然成风。

There is another story about the moon-cakes, which was

concerned with the rebellion against rulers of the Yuan Dynasty (1271 AD — 1368 AD). Stuffed into each moon-cake was a piece of paper with the message "Rise against the rulers on the fifteenth day of the eighth month". The moon-cakes with the message inside were distributed to the residents in the city. On the night of the festival, the rebels successfully attacked and overthrew the government. Since then it became a common practice for the people to celebrate the Mid-Autumn Festival with moon-cakes.

当然，中秋吃月饼，和清明吃粽子一样，它的历史渊源应该另有说法，而世代相传的传说则寄托着人们的一种感情，同样应该受到珍惜。

Of course, eating moon-cakes on the Mid-Autumn Festival, just like eating Zongzi on the Dragon-Boat Festival, ought to have its own origin. But the legends passed down the generations really tell us something valuable of the people's emotions involved in the Mid-Autumn Festival.

中秋节的风俗活动很多，最常见的是全家人团聚在一起，吃一餐团圆饭，然后在皎洁的月光下，赏月，祭月，吃月饼。除此而外，各地还有不少花样，诸如卖兔儿爷、烧斗香、走月亮、放灯、树中秋、舞火龙、曳石等，都曾经给人留下深刻的印象。

There are a good many activities of the Mid-Autumn

Festival, but the most common practice is that all the family members appreciate and worship the moon in the bright moonlight, and eat moon-cakes after having a reunion dinner. There are some special practices in different parts of the country, such as selling Lord Rabbits, burning a *dou* of joss sticks, walking in the moonlight, hanging lanterns, planting Mid-Autumn trees, fire-dragon dances and mill towing, all with deep impressions.

北方民间盛行兔儿爷。佛经里有一个故事，说神仙分别向狐狸、猴、兔求食，狐狸和猴都给了食物，唯独兔子一无所有，它说："你就吃我的肉吧。"然后纵身跳入烈火之中。神仙很是感动，就把兔子送到月宫。兔儿爷是不是就是跳到火里去自焚献身的兔子，这还有待考证。不过至迟在明清的典籍里，就已不乏"兔儿爷”的记载，说人们在中秋节用泥塑成兔形，衣冠踞坐，如人状，儿女祀而拜之。老人回忆，旧时北京东四牌楼一带，每当临近中秋，就会有不少摊贩，专售各式各样的兔儿爷，琳琅满目，煞是好看。人们把兔儿爷买回去，供在祭月的供桌上，或是放在室内，成为一种摆设，小孩子们当然就更加喜爱它了。

The Lord Rabbits are popular in northern China. There is a story in the Buddhist Scriptures that an immortal begged food from a fox, a monkey and a rabbit. They all provided him with food except for the rabbit because he had nothing. But the rabbit jumped into the raging fire after telling the immortal to eat his meat, which moved the immortal so deeply that he sent the rabbit to the Moon Palace. Whether the Lord Rabbit is associated with the story has yet to be proved, but it was really mentioned in the books of the Ming and the Qing dynasties that people moulded a rabbit in clay which was sitting dressed like a man and worshiped by the children. Some aged people recalled that in the former Beijing's Dongsi Pailou, there were many stalls selling a variety of attractive lord rabbits when the Mid-Autumn Festival was around the corner. People put them on the sacrificing tables at home, or put them indoors for decoration. The children of course liked them very much.

中秋斗香，是古代祭月仪礼的衍变。古代帝王都要在中秋节祭月，如今北京的月坛，就是当年留下来的。这种风俗影响到民间，有的地方的商家就会专门制造一种“斗香”出售，四方形，上大下小，纱绢或纸糊成，形似斗，却又装饰得十分漂亮，四角挑灯，里边可以点香烛，家家户户买回去，专供中秋夜祭月用，一时间成为风气，不过如今已经很少见了。

The burning of a *dou* of joss sticks in the Mid-Autumn Festival evolved from the ancient worship of the moon and the Temple of Moon in Beijing was built for the purpose of the emperor's worship on the festival. The custom was so influential that some manufacturers got the idea to sell the *dou* of joss sticks, which was made of paper or silk in the shape of a square like the measuring implement of *dou* in China, which was bigger at the upper part while smaller at the lower part and hung from four corners with beautiful decorations and joss sticks inside. It was a fashion that people brought them home to worship the moon, but they are rarely seen today.

走月亮，又称为踏月、游月、玩月，是妇女们最喜欢的活动。中秋节夜晚，妇女们三五成群，在月色下畅游，有的地方还顺带着要走桥，也颇有情趣。在江南一些地方，还有“摸秋”习俗，这一天到瓜田里去摸个瓜来，放在不育女子的床上，俗信以为可以“求子”。

Walking in the Mid-Autumn moonlight, also known as

Moon-Watching, is a women's favorite event. On the night of the Mid-Autumn Festival, women went out for a walk in groups and sometimes walked over a bridge for fun. In South China, people have a custom of Autumn-Touching. It is said that on that day people would pick up a melon in the field and put it on the bed of a lady who could not be pregnant to make an offer for a son.

中秋夜与元宵夜相似，也往往要挂灯。《武林旧事》里提到，南宋朝廷要在中秋夜到钱塘江里放“一点红”羊皮小水灯数十万盏，这样一种场面，想来是很壮观的。而在广州一带，则有“树中秋”，又称“竖中秋”，则完全是一种民间灯会了。中秋夜，家家挂灯，满城灯火，犹如明星闪烁，把月亮烘托得更加动人。

The Mid-Autumn Festival is similar to the Lantern Festival in hanging lanterns. Mentioned in the book *Wulin Jiushi* (*Old Affairs of Wulin*), it was spectacular that the court of the Southern Song Dynasty put millions of small water lanterns, made of sheep skin, in the Qiantang River. And in the Guangzhou area, there is a custom of celebrating the Mid-Autumn Festival by holding a huge lantern show, which is a big attraction to local citizens. Thousands of different-shaped lanterns are lit, forming a fantastic contrast against the bright moonlight.

在福建霞浦一带，这一天夜里要“曳石”。人们用石块系上绳索，在街上拖拉游戏。据说这是为了纪念抗倭英雄戚继光。

In the area of Xiapu, Fujian Province, people pull the rope tied to a mill stone on the night of the Mid-Autumn Festival to honor Qi Jiguang, the hero of resisting foreign aggressions.

云南傣族要在中秋夜“拜月”。传说天皇的第三个儿子岩尖曾经率领傣族人民打败入侵的外敌，他死后变成了月亮。人们在这天夜晚要准备丰盛的供品，祭奠岩尖，称为“拜月”。鄂伦春族则在空地上放一盆清水，这时候，月亮的倒影便呈现在水盆里，人们用小石子去抛打盆中的月影，俗称“打月亮”。广西的壮族，则在中秋夜祭月神。他们在村口设供桌，桌边竖起一尺多高的树枝，象征社树。老人说，这是月神下凡用的梯子。祭月神的仪式很隆重，包括接神、神人对歌、请神卜卦和送神这样几个程序。

People of the Dai ethnic group in Yunnan Province worship the moon on the night of the Mid-Autumn Festival. The legend goes that the third son of the Emperor of Heaven, Yan Jian, led the people of the Dai ethnic group to defeat the foreign aggressions and was turned into the moon after death. So people got the tribute ready to offer sacrifice to him on that night, which is called the worship of the moon. People of the Oroqen ethnic group have the custom of putting a basin of pure water on the ground and the shadow of the moon is seen in the basin. People could throw stones at the shadow, which is called beating the moon. People of the Zhuang ethnic group in Guangxi Zhuang Autonomous Region worship the Moon Goddess by putting a sacrificing table at the entrance to the village with a one-foot branch against it, which, according to the elders, symbolizes the *She Tree* to be used as a ladder for the God Moon to come to the earth. The ceremony is elaborate, including greeting the God, singing between the God and man, inviting the God to fortune-telling and seeing the God off.

总之，各民族、各个地域民众在中秋节里的一些具体做法会出现种种差异，但是人们对于月圆的企盼和由此引发的对亲人的思念之情，却是相通的。宋代大诗人苏东坡的诗句："但愿人长久，千里共婵娟"，正是对这种情怀的生动写照。只要月亮还在，看来这个中秋节就还得一直过下去了。

To sum up, the celebrating performances vary for different ethnic groups in different parts of China, but what they have in common is that people are expecting the full moon and longing for their relatives. As is said in Su Dongpo's poem in the Song Dynasty that "I wish that we all would have a long life, / And share the bright moon even miles apart." It seems that the celebrations will continue as long as the moon is still bright.

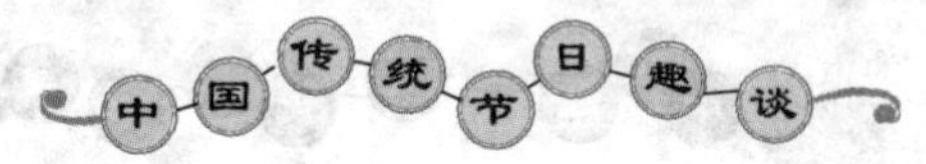

十、重阳节

10. The Double-Ninth Festival

"独在异乡为异客，每逢佳节倍思亲。
遥知兄弟登高处，遍插茱萸少一人。"
A stranger in a strange land, alone I stay;
I get more homesick every festive day.
Brothers climbing a hill afar I see,
They all wear a dogwood spray but me.

唐代大诗人王维的《九月九日忆山东兄弟》诗一向脍炙人口。从这里我们可以窥见，那时候的人们非常看重九月初九这个"佳节"。诗里还提到这一天流行的两种节日风俗：登高和插茱萸。农历九月初九，称为重阳节，民间又称"登高节"、"女儿节"、"重九节"、"九月九"、"茱萸节"、"菊花节"。《易经》中说："以阳爻为九。"九被称为阳数，两九相重，所以称"重九"。两阳相重，又称"重阳"。

The poem *Thinking of My Brothers in Shandong on the Double-Ninth Day* was written by Wang Wei, a great poet in the Tang Dynasty (618 AD — 917 AD). It is a quite popular poem indicating that the Double-Ninth Day was not only valued highly as a joyous festival by the ancient people but also marked with two customs: height-ascending and dogwood-wearing. The ninth day of the ninth lunar month is called the Double-Ninth Festival, along with other popular names, namely, the Height-Ascending Festival, the Daughter's Day, the Chongyang Festival, the Ninth Day of the Ninth Lunar Month, the Dogwood-Wearing Festival, and the Chrysanthemum Festival. According to *Yi Jing* (*The Book of Changes*), the Chinese character *yang* suggests the figure nine and nine is a figure of *yang*. Besides, double means *chong* in Chinese. Thus, with the figure ninth doubled, this day is called the Double-Ninth Festival; with *yang* doubled, this day is also named as the Chongyang Festival.

最早提到"重阳"的，是屈原《远游》诗的"集重阳入帝宫兮"，不过当时是不是已成为节日，还缺乏证据。三国魏文帝曹丕《九日与钟繇书》中则比较明确地提到这是个节日了。书称："岁往月来，忽复九月九日。九为阳数，而日月并应，俗嘉其名，以为宜于长久，故以享宴高会。"说这一天有设宴欢庆，亲朋聚会的风俗。还有一本书也提到这个节日，那就是东晋葛洪《西京杂记》，说汉高祖刘邦的爱妃戚夫人有个侍儿贾佩兰，戚夫人遇害后，贾佩兰被逐出宫，嫁与扶风人段儒为妻。她曾对人说起当年皇宫里的种种风俗，其中就有"九月九日，佩茱萸，食蓬饵，饮菊花酒，令人长寿"。由此可见，这个节日一开始可能是在皇宫中流行，后来"上行下效"，逐渐渗透到了民间，而至迟在汉代就已经很有些名气了。

The first message to mention Chongyang was Qu Yuan's poem *Traveling Faraway*, saying that "Stop in 'Chongyang' (sky) and enter the 'God's palace", but we are still short of convincing evidence concerning whether or not this day was observed as a festival at that time. While *A Letter to Zhong Yao on the Double-Ninth Day* by Cao Pi, Emperor Wen of Wei (220 AD—265 AD) in the Three Kingdoms (220 AD—280 AD), referred to this day as a festival more clearly. It said "As time and tide come and go, the ninth day of the ninth lunar month is approaching again. Since nine is a figure of *yang* and both the date and the month are of ninth, people call it Chongyang in the hope of living

a long life and thus, they always enjoy grand gatherings on this day." These words revealed that people of Wei had already been accustomed to celebrating this day by giving a big banquet and gathering all the relatives and friends. Another book *Miscellaneous Records of the Western Capital*, by Ge Hong in the Eastern Jin Dynasty (317 AD —420 AD), portrayed this festival as follows: Madam Qi, the beloved imperial concubine of Liu Bang, the first emperor of the Han Dynasty, had a maid named Jia Peilan. After Madam Qi died, Jia Peilan was driven out of the palace and married to Duan Ru, a Fufengnese. She once talked about the varieties of customs in the palace in these years, among which was the custom like "On the ninth day of the ninth lunar month, wearing dogwoods, eating cakes, and drinking the chrysanthemum wine can be conducive to longevity". From this custom we can detect clearly that this festival was very popular initially in the imperial palace, then gradually penetrated into the people's life due to their following the superiors' examples, and during the Han Dynasty (206 BC—220 AD), it had become widely known to the populace.

魏晋南北朝的时候，有关重阳节的记载渐渐多了起来。《晋书》里就提到，陶渊明的外祖父孟嘉，重阳节登龙山，只顾观赏美景，一时忘情，竟连山风吹落了他的帽子都还没有察觉。不过当别人嘲笑他时，他却写了篇很好的文章，应对自如，令人钦佩不已。从此便有“龙山落帽”这个典故，用来指称重阳节登高饮酒的风雅事。

While in the Wei, Jin, and Southern and Northern dynasties (220 AD — 581 AD), there were a moderately increasing number of materials recorded concerning the Double-Ninth Festival. As was mentioned in *Chronicles of the Jin Dynasty*, Meng Jia, Tao Yuanming's grandfather, once climbed the Longshan Mountain on the Double-Ninth Festival. He was so lost in appreciating the beautiful scenery that he was not even aware that his cap had been blown away by the wind. However, when laughed at by other people, he, instead, managed to make a wonderful article of it. His replies in the article were so skillful and resourceful that he gained himself endless admirations from the people, bringing about the allusion "the cap falls on the Longshan Mountain" to designate the social graces of height-ascending (mountain-climbing) and wine-drinking on the Double-Ninth Festival.

还有一个传说，影响就更加大些。那是记载在南朝梁吴均《续齐谐记》里的一段传说。说的是东汉时有个汝南人桓景，拜当时一个著名人物费长房为师。据说费长房是个神仙，神通广大，可以驱使鬼神，又能治愈百病，估计他是巫师一类的人物。费长房对桓景说，今年九月初九，将有大灾难降临你的家乡，你要给家里的人都缝一个小袋，里面装上茱萸叶，系在臂上，然后登山，饮菊花酒，就可以躲过这场灾祸了。桓景不敢怠慢，一切照办，在这一天带全家人登山，果然平安无事。傍晚回到家中，发现家里的鸡犬牛羊都莫名其妙地死去了。这样一来，他们愈发相信起费长房的话来。消息不胫而走，众人纷纷仿效，从此便有了九月初九登高避难的风俗。

Another legend was more popular, which was recorded in *Sequel to Tales of Qi Xie*, written by Wu Jun in Liang of the Southern Dynasties (420 AD—589 AD). In the legend, Heng Jing, a Runanese in the Eastern Han Dynasty, acknowledged Fei Changfang as his teacher. It was said that Fei Changfang was a famous person, full of supernatural powers and capable of dispelling ghosts and healing varieties of diseases. Accordingly, he was claimed as sorcerer of a kind. Fei Changfang once said to Heng Jing, "On this Double-Ninth Day, a frightening disaster will approach your hometown. To avoid it, you've got to stitch for each member in your family a small bag filled with the leaves of dogwoods. Then on that day, you, along with your family, should climb a mountain with the bags tied to the arms and drink the chrysanthemum wine." Upon hearing that, Heng Jing hurried to act on whatever Fei Changfang had suggested. As a result, his whole family was safe and sound, only to find all the domestic animals, including chickens, dogs, sheep, and even the powerful oxen, dead mysteriously after they got home at dusk. For this reason, they believed in Fei Changfang even more firmly than before. As the news spread widely, all the people followed their examples and thus, the custom of escaping disasters by ascending a height on the Double-Ninth Day came into being.

当然，这也是一种附会。人们对重阳节风俗的由来无法解释，便生发这样一则故事来。不过，到了这段时间，秋高气爽，倒确实是很适宜人们郊游的。尤其是居住在城镇里的人，相对较为压抑，空气也总是不够新鲜，找个机会到野外走走，是他们的共同心愿。特别是登高望远，更能呼吸到新鲜空气，而且又是锻炼身体的一种好办法，何乐而不为。有人说，九九重阳，九是最大的数字，又与“久”谐音，有着生命长久、健康长寿的象征意义在里边，于是就有了郊游登高，追求健康长寿的种种欲望。

Of course, this is a far-fetched story. It was just because the origin of the custom of the Double-Ninth Festival was beyond people’s explanation that they invented such a legend. Nevertheless, the ninth lunar month, with its clear autumn sky and crisp air, is definitely a good time for outing, especially for people living in cities and towns, who live a life of more pressures and have no fresh air to breathe in. Therefore, they all wish to seek a chance to have a walk in the open country. Ascending a height to enjoy a distant view, in particular, is a very good way for people to breathe in the fresh air and build up a strong constitution. So, why not go ahead with it? As is mentioned above, "double-ninth" suggests "Chongyang" (Double means "Chong" in Chinese) and nine is the biggest figure and a homonym of "jiu", which implies "for ever" in Chinese. Hence, outing and height-ascending are desired by the people for the purpose of achieving both health and longevity.

登高，或许跟古人对大山的崇拜有着某种联系。古人以为大山很神秘，那里蕴藏着无穷的宝物，取之不竭，用之不尽。山里有山神，山神是会保佑人们的。凡此种种，便渐渐地有了对山的崇拜和对山神的崇拜。而每当遇到灾难，特别是像洪水一类的灾难时，人们首先想到的自然是往山上跑。登高和避难，自然而然地联系到了一起。找一个日子，象征性地避一次难，使之成为一种仪式，或许是当时人们的一种想法。按阴阳五行说的解释，重九之日，地气上升，天气下降，天地之气交接，登高则可避不正之气。在这样一种文化心理的熏陶下，重阳登高便脱颖而出了。

Height-ascending is, perhaps, related to the ancestors' worship for the mountains. They always considered the mountains to be fairly mysterious and full of treasures to be consumed. They also believed that there were some mountain gods blessing them. All these beliefs gradually aroused people's worship for the mountains and the mountain gods. Each time disasters happened to them, particularly the floods, the first idea hitting them was to run to the top of a mountain. For this reason, height-ascending and disaster-escaping were naturally associated with each other. Finding a day to escape a token disaster and treating it as a regular ceremony might be a brilliant idea of the people at that time. According to the theory of *yin-yang*, and Wuxing, on the Double-Ninth Day, the air on the earth ascended while the air in the sky descended, and they would meet with each other in this process. So height-ascending enabled the people to be free of the foul air. With people exposed to such cultural psychology, height-ascending on the Double-Ninth Festival eventually found its way to distinction from others.

至于避难和求吉、求长寿，其实也并不矛盾。这不过是一个事物的两个方面罢了。躲避灾难，归根到底也就是祈求平安吉祥。而就一个人的命运来说，长寿是最大的福气，是最佳的吉祥，追求长寿首先当然是要躲避人生道路上各种各样的灾难。在这一点上，重阳节和上巳节有着类似的象征意义，春天到了，万物复苏，古人到野外尽情欢乐，他们首先想到的是祓除，也就是驱赶晦气、躲避灾祸。这就是当初的上巳。秋天到了，古人又想到野外去尽情欢乐一番了，他们首先想到的依旧是避难。当然，避难、祛祟，只是一种仪式，一种例行公事，一种提醒。仪式之后，依旧是欢乐，这也是亘古不变的。《旧唐书·德宗本纪》提到，“汉崇上巳，晋纪重阳”，不同的朝代有不同的风尚，而节日背后所蕴藏着的民众心态，却是惊人地相似。

Just like the two sides of every coin, disaster-escaping and luck-and-longevity-pursuing are not contradictory. Disaster-escaping, in the final analysis, is to pray for safety and fortune. But as far as a person's fate is concerned, longevity is the biggest blessing and the best fortune. To achieve longevity, we must first escape varieties of disasters in our life, which is what the Double-Ninth Festival shares with the Shangsi Festival in their respective symbols. In spring, when all the creatures came back to life, the ancient people would like to enjoy themselves in the open country, with the intention of driving out the ill lucks and avoiding disasters. This showed the way the Shangsi Festival used to be. Similarly, when autumn was around the corner, the ancestors again remembered to entertain themselves in the country, still with the intention of escaping disasters. In a word, disaster-escaping and evil-eliminating were nothing but a kind of ceremonies, mere formalities and remindings. After the ceremony, the people would be as joyous as usual. *The Old Chronicles of the Tang Dynasty: History of Kings of De and Xuan* mentioned "The Shangsi Festival was advocated in the Han Dynasty while the Double-Ninth Festival was recorded in the Jin Dynasty (265 AD—420 AD)." It is true that different dynasties had their distinct prevailing customs, but the people's mentalities

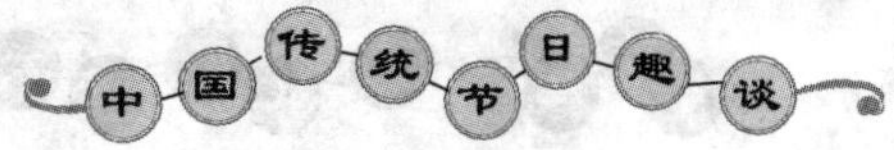

implied in the festivals shared extremely amazing similarities.

有山的地方，登高就是登山。附近没山的地方，登楼、登塔，也就是登高了。

With mountains around, height-ascending refers to mountain-climbing; without mountains nearby, height-ascending means climbing the buildings or towers.

除了登高，这一天里还有好些事要做，当然不同的时空里又会有所差异。归纳起来，插茱萸，饮菊花酒，赏菊，吃重阳糕等等，都别有一番情趣。

Besides height-ascending, there are many other activities, varying from region to region. To sum up, wearing dogwoods, drinking chrysanthemum wine, appreciating chrysanthemums, and eating the Double-Ninth cake have been regarded as special delights for the people.

茱萸是一种有着特殊辛气的常绿小乔木，一般以为可以用来驱蚊杀虫。古人进一步夸大它的功能，以为可以祛一切恶浊之气，这当然已经带有某种巫术的味道了。不过茱萸是药，倒是不成问题的。如今常见的“十全大补丸”、“六味地黄丸”里，也总是会用到这一味药材的，当年风俗，将茱萸的树叶和果实采来，装入小布袋，佩戴在身上；或是在鬓发之间插一株茱萸；或是将茱萸泡在酒里饮用，大概都是把它当做一种预防疾病的措施。后来，只是因为这种植物比较难以采摘得到，一般人觉得麻烦，渐渐地，它便淡出了人们的记忆。倒是前面提到王维的那首诗，则总是在提醒着后人，当年的重阳节可是要插茱萸的呵。后来有的地方流行用彩帛剪成茱萸形状，相互赠送和佩戴，则是古风的一种衍变。

As for the dogwood, it is a species of small evergreen arbor with a special hot smell. It is generally believed that the dogwood can be used to drive away mosquitoes and kill harmful insects. While for the ancient people, the function of the dogwood was exaggerated even to the extent of eliminating all the evil spirits, somewhat sorcery-like. It is certain that the dogwood is a kind of herbal medicine and serves as one ingredient of the medicines "Bolus of Ten Powerful Tonics" and "Pill of Six Ingredients with Rehmannia" frequently seen today. As a traditional custom, the people either picked the leaves and fruits, put them in a small sack and carried it with them, or worn them in the hair on the temples and soaked them in the wine for drinking. Maybe all these were due to the fact that the people then treated the dogwood as one means to prevent various diseases. Later on, as people found it difficult and troublesome to pick dogwoods, this custom died out from people's memory. In fact, it was Wang Wei's poem mentioned above that constantly reminded us of the custom on the Double-Ninth Day in those years that the people ought to wear dogwoods. Afterwards, the people in some areas developed the traditional customs by presenting and wearing colorful silken dogwoods.

九月，古人又称“菊月”。这时候百花凋零，唯有菊花傲霜挺立，所以历来受到人们的赞叹。文人爱菊，往往以菊喻人，欣赏它那高洁的品格。而老百姓喜欢它，则又多了一层实用的成分，那是说菊花也可以治病。特别是有一种白菊花，是可以泡茶喝的，据说可以清凉明目。大约在汉代的时候，人们就已经开始用菊花酿酒了。九月，菊花盛开，选用可以食用的甘菊或白菊，煮成汁拌和曲米一起酿酒，到明年九月九饮用，俗信则以为可以辟邪。

The ninth lunar month was also called the Chrysanthemum Month by the ancient people. In this month, all the other flowers withered, while chrysanthemums, flourishing against the frost, were thus highly praised. Literary men loved the chrysanthemum for its noble and unsullied character, and frequently compared chrysanthemums in their writings to the noble-minded people. However, the common people love chrysanthemums for their medical functions. For instance, the tea soaked with white chrysanthemums was believed to be able to cool and clear our eyes. It was said that people in the Han Dynasty began to make wine with chrysanthemums. As the chrysanthemums were at their best

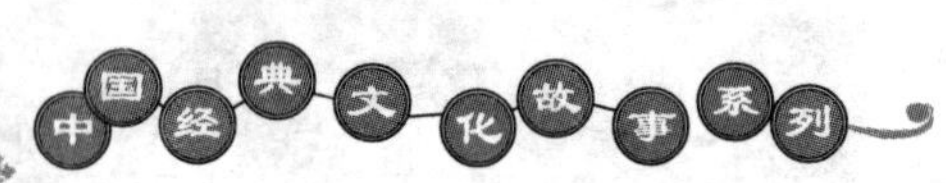

in the ninth lunar month, people would pick the edible sweet chrysanthemums and the white chrysanthemums and then made wines with the juices of the boiled chrysanthemums and grains, which would not be drunk until the same day next year. This was also a popular custom of driving away the evil spirits.

古代还有把菊花簪在头上的风俗，也有辟邪的用意在里面。北京一带，当年在重阳节的时候还要把菊花的枝叶贴在自家的门窗上，据说也是为了祛除凶秽，迎来吉祥。

Another custom in the old days was to wear chrysanthemums in the hair so as to eliminate evil spirits. It was said that people in the Beijing area stuck the chrysanthemum leaves to their windows and doors to get rid of misfortunes and filth and welcome good lucks.

赏菊，也由来已久。六朝时候，士大夫中间就有赏菊的风尚，君王则还会把菊花当做一种赏赐，赠送给臣下。陶渊明爱菊，“采菊东篱下，悠然见南山”，众所周知。他还有一首诗则说：“菊花如我心，九月九日开。客人知我意，重阳一同来。”就和重阳节风俗贴得更紧了。到了唐代，重阳赏菊已蔚然成风。《辇下岁时记》说：“长安宫掖在九月九日争插菊花”，其实民间也是如此，杜牧的诗句：“尘世难逢开口笑，菊花须插满头归”，便是明证。还有一位农民起义领袖黄巢，也留下了一首咏菊的诗：“待到秋

来九月八，我花开后百花杀。冲天香阵透长安，满城尽带黄金甲。”大气磅礴，给人留下的印象就更深了。

Chrysanthemum-appreciating has a long history. Ever since the Six Dynasties, the literati and officials took delights in appreciating the chrysanthemums and the emperors even granted their officials chrysanthemums as rewards. Tao Yuanming loved chrysanthemums, with his lines "I pluck hedge-side chrysanthemums with pleasure / and see the tranquil southern mountain in leisure" well-known in China. Another poem of his was more closely linked with the customs of the Double-Ninth Festival, which reads,

"Satisfied am I with all the chrysanthemums,
Blooming on this Double Ninth Day.
Considerate are my guests of my feelings,
Visiting me together all the way."

By the Tang Dynasty (618 AD—907 AD), chrysanthemum-appreciating on the Double-Ninth Festival had become a common social practice. Just as *Nian Xia Suishiji* (*Records of Events Outside the Carriage*) noted, "In the palace of Chang'an city, people competed to wear chrysanthemums on the Double-Ninth Day". It was also no exception among the common people. Du Mu's verse "Hardly meet laughter in this world / Come back with chrysanthemums throughout the hair" is a good case in point. Besides, Huang Chao, leader of the peasant uprising, also left us an ode to the chrysanthemum:

"Until on the Double Ninth Festival,
my flowers are blooming while others are faded.
With the drifting fragrance of the chrysanthemum flower,
the whole Chang'an city looks like armed with golden armor."

The poem was of such tremendous momentum that it had left a deep impression on the people.

重阳糕的习俗也很有趣。据说它也跟“登高”有关，有的地方无山可登，那里的人们便又想出了一个妙招，说“糕”和“高”同音，那就吃糕吧。有人还把糕做成了九层，就更像是座小山了。糕上再捏出两只小羊来，也是用来象征“重阳”的。还有的在糕上插彩色小旗，点上小蜡烛。彩旗大概是从茱萸衍变出来的。点上灯烛，也有“登”的意思在里头，点灯的糕，岂不是“登高”吗？重阳糕一般都做得很精致，有的还嵌入了蜜饯、枣脯，愈发可口。在北方，则又有重阳节吃羊肉的食俗。《燕京岁时记》里就提到在重阳节要“烤肉分糕”。

The interesting custom of eating the Double-Ninth cake is, likewise, considered to be related to "height-ascending". In regions without mountains to climb, some people struck upon a wonderful idea of eating the "Gao"(cake), for "Gao" is a homonym of 'height" in Chinese. Some people made the cake in nine layers in order to resemble a small hill. Some people molded two lambs on the cake (for lamb is a homonym of "yang" in Chinese) to symbolize "Chongyang", while other people dotted the cake with some colorful banners and small lighted candles. Maybe the colorful banners were derived from the dogwoods and the lighted candles sounded like "climb" or "ascend" in Chinese. In view of this, the lighted cake doubtlessly symbolized "height-ascending." The Double-Ninth cakes were made quite delicately. Some were embedded with preserves and jujube's fruits, more delicious to the taste. In the northern areas, eating mutton on the Double Ninth Day was another custom. *Yanjing Suishiji* (*Yanjing Age in Mind*) described it as "mutton-roasting and cake-sharing".

古代，重阳节还是骑马练兵、讲武习射的节日。有人说，重阳糕就曾经是当年发给三军士兵的一种干粮。在东北、内蒙一带，历史上就盛行过重阳节打围、骑射的习俗。有的地方，还会在这一天放风筝。在华北、东北的一些地方，这一天要接已经出嫁的女儿回娘家，大家在一起吃菊花糕，俗称“女儿节”。蒙古、彝、布依、白、土家、侗、畲、仫佬等兄弟民族，也在这一天过节，他们的节日名称和风俗活动则会有所不同。

In the old times, the Double-Ninth Festival was, at the same time, the festival of horse riding, soldier training, gongfu instructing, and shooting practicing. It is said that the Double-Ninth cakes were supplied to the armies as army provisions.

In some areas in the northeast of China and Inner Mongolia, the customs of animal encircling, hunting and shooting on the horsebacks prevailed in former days. On this day, people in some regions would fly kites, while in other areas of north and northeast China, the families with married daughters would welcome them back home and share the chrysanthemum cakes. Thus, this day is also called the Daughter's Day. Such ethnic groups as the Mongolian, Yi, Buyi, Bai, Tujia, Dong, She and Mulao also celebrated this festival too, but with different names and customs.

重阳节风俗，在人们心目中影响最大的，还是登高，由登高所联想到的，就是健身、长寿。如今，人们又把重阳节当做“老人节”、“敬老节”。每到这个时候，社会上总要掀起一股热潮，提倡尊敬老人、照顾老人。说起来，尊老爱老，孝顺父母，是中华民族的传统美德。发扬这种美德，和重阳佳节的节令情调倒也是蛮融洽的。

Actually, the most influential custom deep in the people's hearts on this day is still height-ascending because it is associated with body-building and life-prolonging. People nowadays also begin to spend the Double-Ninth Festival as the Seniors' Day. On this day each year, activities will be set off to advocate respecting and caring for the old people. After all, it is China's traditional virtue to respect the old, love the

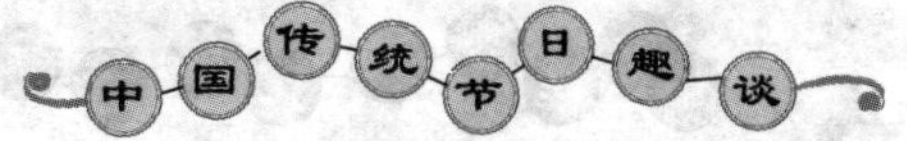

young and to be filial to their parents. There is no denying that promoting and developing these virtues are perfectly harmonious with the cheerful atmospheres of the Double-Ninth Festival.

十一、冬至

11. The Winter Solstice

冬至，是二十四节气之一。这一天是一年当中白天最短，黑夜最长的一天。过了冬至，白天一天比一天长。冬至的时间是立冬以后的46天，按阳历，一般在12月22日前后。

The Winter Solstice, one of the twenty four seasonal division points, falls on the forty-sixth day after the Beginning of Winter, around each December 22nd according to the solar calendar. On this day, the northern hemisphere experiences the shortest daytime and the longest nighttime and after this day, days will become longer and longer.

作为传统节日，冬至节又称"冬节"、"交冬"、"亚冬"，曾经也是很隆重的。《周礼》中提到，"以冬日至，致天神人鬼"。说的是周代在这一天要有祭祀仪式。汉代则成为节日，这天前后，人们要安身静体，百官绝事不听政，择吉辰而后省事。有一种说法，古代曾经实行过一种历法，是把冬至当做一年的开始，过冬至犹如过年。后来历法改了，元旦定在另外一个日子，冬至的重要性才逐渐下降。不过一直到唐宋时，冬至还是和元旦一样重要的。《东京梦华录》卷十"冬至"中提到，这一天，"庆贺往来，一如年节"。直至近现代，民间还有俗谚称："冬至大如年"，说它是和过年一样重要的。民间称这一天是“过小年”，又称“贺冬”。

As a traditional festival, the Winter Solstice is also called the Winter Festival, the Turning of the Winter, and the Sub-winter, which had ever been quite ceremonious. *Rites of the Zhou* had a record of “The Winter Solstice is the day to offer sacrifices to gods and ancestors”, indicating that in the Zhou Dynasty (1046 BC—221 BC), people had to hold a ceremony to offer sacrifices to gods and ancestors on this day. In the Han Dynasty (206 BC—220 AD), this day was an established festival. Around this day, people should stop doing things; officials wouldn’t administer affairs of state until a lucky time and day. It was said that a calendar had been laid down to make the Winter Solstice the beginning of a year and the people spent this day as they did a new year. Afterwards, the calendar was changed and the Winter Solstice became less important after the New Year’s Day was transferred to another day. But the Winter Solstice remained as important as the New Year’s Day up to the Tang (618 AD—907 AD) and Song dynasties (960 AD—1279 AD). According to Volume 10 of *The Eastern Capital: A Dream of Splendors Past on the Winter Solstice*, “(People) celebrate and exchange friendly visits just as they do in festivals or on the New Year’s Day.” Even in modern times, people still have a common saying “The Winter Solstice is as grand as the New Year’s Day”, meaning that it is as important as the New Year's Day. Accordingly, people called this day "the Sub-New Year" as well as "Winter-Celebration".

正因为如此，冬至的节日风俗活动，大致上也就和过年相仿。旧时，这一天官府和学校放假，商业歇市，作坊停工，人们穿新衣，亲友间相互送礼宴请，家中则祭祀祖先，然后全家聚餐等等。清代的《清嘉录》中，提到江南的冬至节，相互送礼的人“提筐担盒，充斥道路。俗呼‘冬至盘’”。别有一番景象。

It is just because of these that there are many customs for the Winter Solstice similar to those for the New Year. On this day in the old times, all the local authorities and schools had a day off; the businesses were stopped; the workshops were closed; people wore new clothes; presents and dinners were offered among relatives and friends. While at home, people would offer sacrifices to their ancestors and then had a dinner party. *Qing Jia Lu* (*Records of Jiaqing Period of the Qing Dynasty*) had a record that in the areas on the South of the Changjiang River, "The streets were crowded with people who carried gifts of baskets or boxes called Plates on the Winter Solstice", which was really a unique view.

冬至的节令食品，最常见的是馄饨。有“冬至馄饨夏至面”的俗谚。这里也有一些有趣的传说。

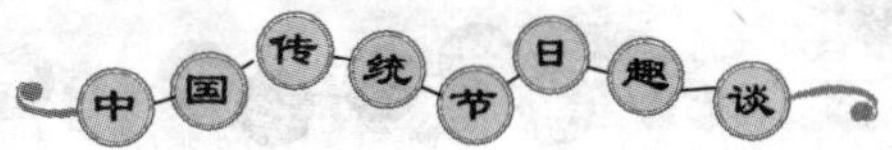
中国传统节日趣谈

Just as the old saying goes, "People eat Wonton (dumpling) soup on the Winter Solstice and noodles on the Summer Solstice", the popular food for the Winter Solstice is Wonton, about which there are two very interesting legends.

一说，春秋战国时，吴王夫差打败越国后，得意忘形，迷恋于歌舞酒色之中而不能自拔。冬至节，看着满桌的山珍海味却一点儿胃口也没有了。西施就亲自下厨，为他做出了一道新颖的点心来。夫差一尝，大加赞赏，问西施，这是什么点心？西施心中暗暗好笑，心想这个昏君成天昏昏沉沉，糊里糊涂，真是有些浑沌不开，于是随口说了声："馄饨。"从此以后，这种点心传入民间，也就有了这么一个名字。

The first legend took place during the Spring and Autumn Period (770 BC—476 BC) and Warring States Periods (220 AD — 280 AD). Fu Chai, King of Wu, got dizzy with his success in defeating the kingdom Yue and thus, was indulged in the song, dance, wine, and women. But on the Winter Solstice, he had no appetite for the whole table of nice dishes of every kind. Finally, Xi Shi made a novel course of dim sum for him, which was quite agreeable to his taste. So he sang high praise for Xi Shi and inquired her of its name. "So ridiculous, so fatuous and foolish a ruler he is!" Xi Shi thought to herself, "Every day he is dizzy and clumsy." Therefore, "Wonton," answered Xi Shi spontaneously. From then on, this kind of dim sum, named as Wonton, penetrated into people's life.

一说，汉朝时，匈奴经常骚扰边疆。匈奴部落中有浑氏、屯氏两个首领，凶狠之极。百姓对这两个人恨之入骨，就用肉馅包在面粉擀成的薄皮里，放进沸水中去煮，取其谐音为“馄饨”，以解心头之恨。

The second legend says that during the Han Dynasty (206 BC — 220 AD), the Huns often harassed the border areas, among whom were the two extremely fierce leaders named Hun Shi and Tun Shi. The populace hated them to the guts, so they packed the meat stuffing with powder wrappers and boiled them in hot water. They named this kind of food "Huntun" (Wonton) in order to relieve their enormous hatred.

当然，这两种传说无非是附会而已，吃馄饨时说说这种掌故，则自有一种乐趣。时至今日，馄饨已十分普及，一年四季都吃，也并非只在冬至这一天吃了。至于冬至的节日食俗，各地也不尽一致，江南一带则要在冬至夜吃赤豆糯米饭。老人说，冬至特别长，要吃饱一点，似乎也顺理成章。也有的地方吃汤圆。而在陕西关中一带，旧时还有“冬至敬师”的习俗，这一天，学生和家长们要给教师送礼，帮老师收拾房间，然后向教师敬酒，师生围坐在一起，讲故事，猜谜语，唱小曲，其情浓浓，令人难忘。

Of course, these legends are nothing but farfetched

conclusions. But it is a great pleasure for people to chatter about these anecdotes when eating Wonton. Up to now, Wonton is quite popular, which is not limited to the Winter Solstice, instead, it is available throughout the year. As for the dietary custom, it varies from region to region. For example, in the areas in the South of the Changjiang River, people eat the cooked glutinous rice mixed with red beans on the evening of the Winter Solstice. The old men always say that people should eat a bit more this day because its daytime is too long. These words sound reasonable and logical. Residents of some other places also eat Tangyuan. While in some areas of the central Guanzhong Plain, people had the custom of "paying respect to teachers on the Winter Solstice" in the old times. It was the very day for students and their parents to give gifts to the teachers, help them clean rooms, and then drink a toast to them. In addition, they sat round, telling stories, guessing riddles, and singing songs together. The deep affection was really unforgettable.

与冬至相关的，还有“数九”，又称“九九”，也颇为别致。冬至以后，九九八十一天，人们将其分成九个段落，每一段落为九天，依次定名为头九、二九、三九，直到九九。通常，三九是最冷的时候，俗称“冷在三九”，而到了九九，就已经寒尽春来，又有“九九艳阳天”的说法。为了便于记忆，各地都有歌诀流行，

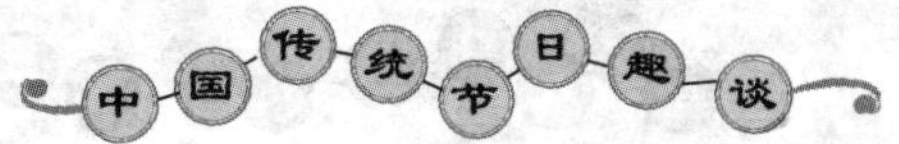

俗称“九九歌”。比如，北方民间的一首“九九歌”就唱道：“未从数九先数九。一九二九，冰上可行走。三九四九，掩门叫黄狗。五九六九，开门缩颈走。七九河开。八九雁来。九九又一九，犁牛遍地走。”既形象生动，又让人记住了冬天的天气规律，可谓民众智慧的结晶。

It is also interesting to know that the Nine Periods or the Nine Nine-day Periods are, likewise, related to the Winter Solstice. After this day, people divide the following eighty-one days into nine periods, each of which is nine days. The first period is called the first nine-day period, and then followed by the second nine-day period, the third nine-day period and so on, up to the ninth nine-day period. Usually, the third nine-day period is the coldest time of the year, so we've got another expression "The coldest time is in the third nine-day period". But, when the ninth nine-day period approaches, coldness will be driven far away by the warm spring. Hence, that "The ninth nine-day period is full of bright spring days" is a vivid expression for that view. To make it easy to remember, every locality has its popular song, called "Song of the Nine Nine-day Periods." Take the popular folk song in the North of China for example:

"It is not in the nine nine-day periods yet,

But we count them in order.

In the first and second nine-day periods,
On the ice you can walk.
In the third and fourth nine-day periods,
With the door latched, you call the yellow dog.
In the fifth and sixth nine-day periods,
You open the door and walk, with the neck short.
In the seventh nine-day period,
The river runs without big ices to block.
In the eighth nine-day period,
The wild geese fly back, in a large flock.
In the ninth nine-day period,
Everywhere in the fields will the ploughing oxen walk."

The song is not only vivid to life but also makes it simple for the people to memorize the law of the winter's weather, which is definitely the crystallization of people's wisdom.

古代，民间还流行“画九”，用有趣的图或文字来记录“九九”的日程和天气变化规律。一般称之为“九九消寒图”，或是画梅花，或是画圆圈，或是填影格字，贴在墙上，每天涂一笔，九九八十一天到了，图画或是图中的文字也就全涂满了，煞是有趣。

In the old times, another custom of "Drawing the Nine Nine-day Periods" was quite popular among the people, that is, people noted down the schedule of "the Nine Nine-day

Periods" and the law of the changes of the weather by drawing interesting pictures or characters, generally called "Pictures of the Nine Nine-day Periods", or by drawing some plum blossoms or circles, or by filling in some characters on the model calligraphy sheet. They pasted these pictures on the wall and scribbled one touch on them each day. Thus, when the eighty-first day came, all the pictures or the characters of the picture would be completed correspondingly. This is really very interesting.

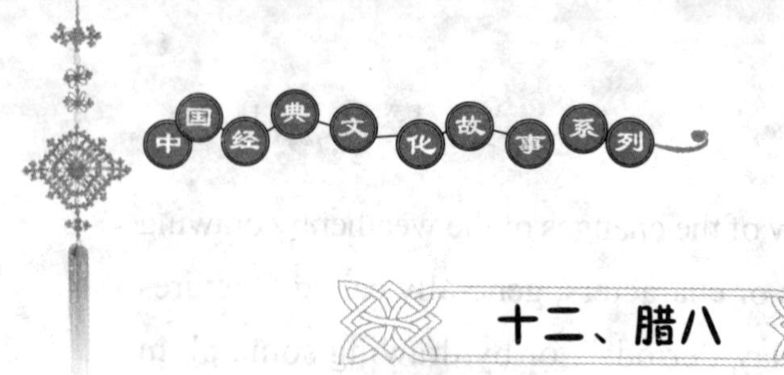

十二、腊八

12. The Laba Festival

农历十二月初八，俗称“腊八”，佛教徒则称之为“佛祖成道节”。

Traditionally, the eighth day of the twelfth lunar month is the Laba Festival, which is well-known as a celebration of the day when Buddha achieved supreme enlightenment.

腊，原先是一种古老的祭礼。农业社会里，人们一年四季都很忙碌，一直要到十二月，才有了些空闲。这时候他们便要举行盛大的祭奠，来祭祀祖先，表示对祖先的感激之情，并且祈求祖先在新的一年里能继续保佑他们。这种祭奠往往需要猎取禽兽作为牺牲。“腊者，猎也”。古时这两个字是相通的。这种在十二月里举行盛大祭礼的风俗大约在周代便已形成。《左传》、《史记》这些书里都有记载。

Originally, *La* referred to the sacrificial rites held in the twelfth lunar month when people stopped their yearly farm work and offered preys (the Chinese characters for prey and La were interchangeable then) to their ancestors, showing their gratitude and asking for blessings. According to *Shiji* (*Historical Records)* and *Zuozhuan* (*Zuo's Commentary*) this

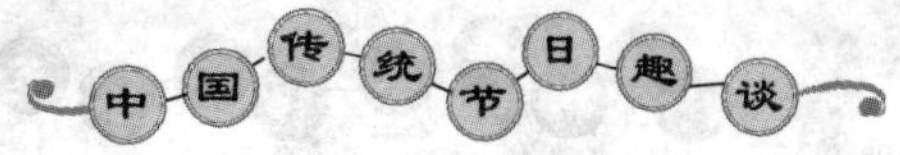

custom of holding sacrificial rites in the twelfth lunar month took shape far back in the Zhou Dynasty (1046 BC—221 BC).

一开始的时候，只说是要在十二月里举行祭礼，所以称十二月为腊月，但腊日究竟是哪一天，似乎并没有定下来。只说十二月是腊月，或说是岁终腊祭，总之还有些含糊。汉代，确定冬至后的第三个戌日为“腊日”，不过具体日期还是很难计算，也不好记。大约到了南北朝，《荆楚岁时记》中才有了明确记载：“十二月八日为腊日”。古人的祭祀，总不外乎两大目的，一是祈福求寿，一是避灾祛祟。《荆楚岁时记》中还提到“腊鼓”，说这一天人们要“击细腰鼓，戴胡头，及作金刚力士以逐疫”，这就是一种在驱逐巫术基础上衍变而成的民间歌舞表演了。这里提到戴面具，看起来是“傩仪”的一种。

At that time the twelfth month was called the month of La because of the ceremony held then. “Lari” namely “Laba”, however, was perhaps not decided yet. It seemed inappropriate to define the twelfth month or the ceremony held then as “Lari”. In the Han Dynasty (206 BC — 220 AD), “Lari” fell on the day three weeks after Winter Solstice, which was actually hard to pin down or remember. Until about the Southern and Northern Dynasties (420 AD — 581 AD) there appeared records in *Jingchu Suishiji* (*Festivals in the Jingchu Area*) that the date of “Lari” was fixed on the eighth day of the twelfth lunar month. The ancient people offered sacrifices to their ancestors mainly to pray for good health and longevity or to ward off disasters and evil spirits. According to *Jingchu Suishiji* on the Laba Festival, people played waisted drums (known as the La Drum) and wore masks acting the Buddha's warrior attendants to ward off illness.

This folk dance is derived from the practice of removing curses and spells. Here wearing the mask is one of the Nuo rituals (*nuo*, to exorcise evil spirits).

这一天还要煮粥来吃，粥的花样也很别致，通常是把糯米和许多种杂粮掺在一起煮成，俗称“腊八粥”。

Another tradition of the Laba Festival is eating porridge.

Though there are various kinds of porridge, traditionally the porridge is prepared with glutinous rice and coarse cereals, known as Laba rice porridge.

至迟在南宋时候，腊八粥就已十分盛行。《武林旧事》说：“（腊月）八日，则寺院及人家用胡桃、松子、乳蕈、柿栗之类作粥，谓之腊八粥。”《梦粱录》也说：“此月八日，寺院谓之腊八。大刹等寺，俱设五味粥，名曰腊八粥。”清代吴存楷《江乡节物诗》，又一次提到腊八粥，诗前小序称：“亦名七宝粥，本僧家斋供，今则居家者亦为之矣。”时至今日，一些寺庙里依旧保持这个传统，每年到了农历十二月初八这一天，总要烧上几大锅腊八粥，施舍给大家吃。旧时，一些有钱人家也会在这一天做善事，烧些腊八粥来接济穷苦百姓。久而久之，许多普通人家则纷纷效仿，索性在自己家里烧上一大锅别具风味的腊八粥，让大伙儿吃个痛快。不同的地域，又会形成不同的特色，诸如淮南的薏米粥、黑龙江的小黄米粥、杭州的藕粥，都颇有些名气。如今则有罐装食品“八宝粥”，也是在继承传统基础上的一种创新。

Laba rice porridge had become popular by the Southern Song Dynasty (1127 AD — 1279 AD). According to *Wu Lin Jiu Shi* (*Old Affairs of Wulin*), on the eighth of the twelfth lunar month, Laba rice porridge was cooked in houses and temples, containing walnuts, pine nuts, mushrooms, persimmon nuts, etc. According to *Meng Liang Lu* (*Record of the Golden Millet Dream*), the eighth day of the twelfth lunar

month was called Laba in temples. In all big Buddhist temples Laba rice porridge was prepared with five ingredients. Wu Cunkai of the Qing Dynasty (1644 AD — 1911 AD) also mentioned Laba rice porridge in the preface to his writing *Jiang Xiang Jie Wu Shi* that Laba rice porridge, also called Qibao (Seven Treasure) porridge, was originally offered to the Buddha in temples, later becoming a popular dish among common people. Nowadays the tradition is still followed in some temples. On every Laba Festival, pots of porridge are prepared and offered to people as alms. In old times rich people would give Laba rice porridge to the poor in charity. Gradually many people followed suit. Laba rice porridge has its local characteristics, such as the porridge made of Job's tears seeds in the southern part of Anhui Province, the millet porridge in Heilongjiang Province, the lotus seed porridge in Hangzhou, which are all very famous. Based on the traditional cooking, canned porridge namely Babao (Eight Treasure) porridge has been developed.

为什么要在这一天吃这样的一种粥？据说有好几种说法：

一种说法，是说佛教的创始人释迦牟尼在成佛之前，曾经游历印度的名山大川，以探究人生哲理。一次，他又饥又饿，酷热难熬，昏倒在地，是一位牧女用自己的午饭救了他。这午饭是用牛马等乳汁和米粟煮在一起而成的粥，称为“乳糜”。释迦牟尼吃了之后恢复了体力，这一天正是腊月初八。所以每逢这一天，佛寺僧众都要诵经演法，取香谷和各种果实煮粥，以示纪念。佛门又认为一切众生都是“未来佛”，都应该供养，所以总是将腊八粥广为施舍。后来民间竞起仿效，渐成风俗。清人顾禄《清嘉录》称：“八日为腊八，居民以菜果入米煮粥，谓之腊八粥。或有馈自僧尼者，名曰佛粥。”唐人李福《腊八粥》诗云：“腊月八日粥，传自梵王国。七宝美调和，五味香糁入。用以供伊蒲，藉之作功德。”因为腊八粥有着一段不寻常的历史，所以受到佛教界的普遍重视，甚至以为这是一种药。《释氏稽古略》卷三载五代齐已《粥疏》，就给了它高度评价：“粥名良药，佛所称扬；义冠三种，功标十利。”

Legends about the origin of Laba rice porridge abound. One of the legends says that when on his way into the high Indian mountains in his quest for understanding and enlightenment, Sakyamuni, founder of Buddhism, grew tired and hungry. Exhausted from days of walking, he passed into unconsciousness. A shepherdess found him there and fed him her lunch — porridge made with beans, rice and milk. Sakyamuni was thus able to continue his journey. That day was the eighth of the twelfth lunar month. Ever since, Sutras were chanted in the temples and rice porridge with beans, nuts and dried fruit was prepared for the Buddha on that day. Buddhists believed that everyone was Buddha of the Future and should be respected, so they offered Laba porridge to

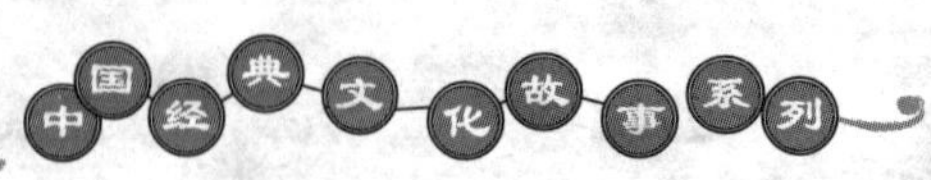

everyone. Later this practice was followed by common people and with the passage of time it developed into a custom. Gu Lu of the Qing Dynasty mentioned in his *Qing Jia Lu* (*Records of Jiaqing Period of the Qing Dynasty*) that on the Laba Festival people made porridge with rice and beans and called it Laba rice porridge. Porridge was also offered by monks and nuns and they called it Buddha's porridge. Li Fu of the Tang Dynasty (618 AD—907 AD) once wrote a poem titled *Laba Rice Porridge*: Laba rice porridge, introduced by Buddhists, containing seven ingredients and flavored by five spices, is very delicious; offered as a vegetarian dish, it spreads the teachings of Buddhism. Connected with such an unusual story, Laba rice porridge had received universal attention. It was even considered as a drug. As indicated in the essay *On Porridge* in Vol. 3 of *Outline of Historical Researches into the Sakya Family Lineage*, the porridge, which is highly thought of by Buddhists, is a good medicine with three benefits and ten effects.

另一种说法，则与明太祖朱元璋有关。据说朱元璋年轻时以放牛为生，饥饿难挨，掘鼠洞掘出不少五谷杂粮，熬粥充饥。后来做了皇帝，吃腻了山珍海味，在腊八这一天忽然想起了当年吃的这种粥，让御厨照样做了送上去，果然别有风味，于是赐名“腊八粥”，传遍了天下。

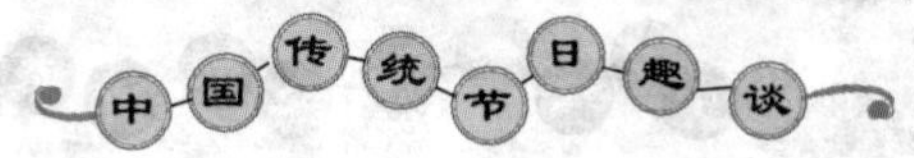

Another story about Laba rice porridge has something to do with Zhu Yuanzhang, Emperor Taizu of the Ming Dynasty (1368 AD—1644 AD). It is said that when he was a cowboy he had to feed himself by cooking porridge with grains dug from the rat holes. Later when he became the emperor, he got fed up with all delicious foods. On the Laba Festival he remembered the porridge he had had as a boy and ordered his cook to make it according to his recipe, which turned out extremely good. The porridge with the name Laba rice porridge, became popular throughout the country.

还有一种说法也挺有趣的，就记载在明代李时珍《本草纲目·谷部》“赤豆”条，说是当年怒触不周山的那个共工氏有七个不肖之子，死后做了疫鬼，肆无忌惮，为所欲为，却偏偏害怕赤豆，所以人们相传在腊八日要做赤豆粥，用来打鬼。说是赤豆粥，其实要放进去好多东西，通常先是将赤豆、白云豆、绿豆、大麦等洗净，放水煮半熟，再放入大米、小米、黄米、高粱等，先用旺火，再用温火，把粥炖熟。吃时加糖，或拌以煮熟的红枣、栗子，还有在粥里放莲子、薏米、菱角米、白果、桂圆的，那就愈发讲究了。据说当年吃“腊八粥”还有一种仪式，先是打鬼，然后再吃粥。久而久之，大家心照不宣，觉得这个打鬼的仪式似乎有点玄乎，不做也罢，就一门心思吃起粥来。

There is still another interesting story, which was recorded by Li Shizhen of the Ming Dynasty in his work *Compendium*

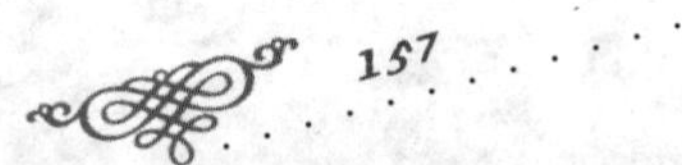

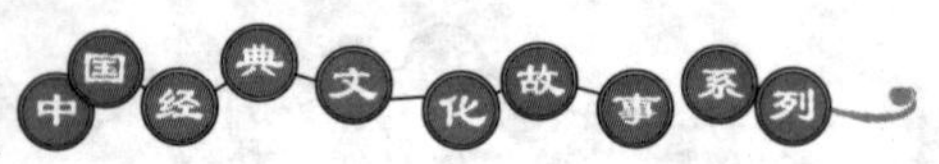

of Materia Medica: Grain Section to explain "red bean". It goes like this: Gong Gong (A red-haired giant monster of half man and half snake, who started a war for power against the god of Zhuan Xu. Defeated, he flied into a rage and hit his humongous head upon the Buzhou Mountain, which was the pillar supporting the sky) had seven unworthy sons, who turned into ghosts of plague after death. They did whatever they liked and would stop at nothing except the red bean. In order to drive them away people passed down the tradition of making red bean porridge. The porridge actually had many ingredients. Red beans, white kidney beans, green beans and barley grains were cleaned and half cooked first. Then it was cooked again with rice, millet, glutinous millet and sorghum. At the start, the flame must be high, but the fire was then turned down to let the porridge simmer. The porridge was then eaten with sugar or cooked dates and chestnuts. Sometimes lotus seeds, Job's tears seeds, water caltrop pulp, ginkgo and longan pulp were added to make it even more tasteful. It was said that Laba rice porridge was eaten after the ceremony of driving ghosts away. Gradually it became an unspoken understanding among people that the ceremony was somewhat ridiculous and unhelpful, therefore they just ate the porridge without the ceremony.

吃腊八粥的说法很不一致，我们似乎也不必去强求一致。说到底这也只不过是人们对于风俗的一种解释罢了。总之，腊八粥是人民大众的一种集体创造，起初它可能还没这么好吃，放进去煮的花色品种也没这么多，后来大家集思广益，群策群力，你加一点，他添一点，就愈发精彩起来。清代《燕京岁时记》里也提到了“腊八粥”的煮法，那就更加复杂而别致。如今的年轻人只知道八宝粥，却不知道它起初叫“七宝粥”，又叫“腊八粥”，还有这么多讲究。如今知道了这些典故，再吃起来恐怕就格外有滋味了。

As indicated above, origins about Laba rice porridge vary greatly, and it is unnecessary to decide which one is more reasonable, since they are just our understanding of the customs. Anyway, Laba rice porridge has been developed collaboratively. It might not necessarily be so delicious as it is now, nor did its ingredients vary so much. But as four eyes see more than two, it was enriched little by little. In *Yanjing Suishiji* (*Yanjing Age in Mind*) written during the Qing Dynasty, the cooking method of Laba rice porridge was also mentioned, which seemed even more complicated and delicate. Nowadays young people only know about Babao (Eight Treasure) porridge, but not its original name Qibao (Seven Treasure) porridge or Laba rice porridge, not to mention the stories behind it. Now that the people know the stories, it would be different when they eat Laba rice porridge again.

十三、藏历年

13. The Tibetan New Year

藏历年，藏语称为“洛萨尔”，是藏族同胞的新年。自从使用藏历，就有了这个节日，大约已有九百多年历史了。拉萨一带，以藏历正月一日为节日；昌都一带，以藏历十一月一日为节日；楚河以南地区，则以藏历十二月一日为节日，各地有所不同。

The Tibetan New Year, known as Losar in Tibetan, is the New Year for the Tibetans. Since the Tibetan calendar was used, people have got this festival for over 900 years. The people of different regions celebrate this festival on different dates. For example, by the lunar Tibetan calendar, this festival falls on the first day of the first month for the people of (or nearby) Lhasa, while for those people of (or nearby) Changdu and the southern areas of Chuhe, the festival falls on the first day of the eleventh month and the first day of the twelfth month respectively.

和汉族过新年一样，藏族同胞非常重视这个节日。他们大多提前半个多月就要动手准备过年，家家户户操办年货，煎油果子，准备手抓羊肉、酥油茶、奶茶、青稞酒等节日食品。以拉萨一带为例，十二月二十九日晚饭前，人们要在打扫干净的灶房正中墙上，用干面粉撒成吉祥图案，在大门上用石灰粉画象征吉祥、永恒的“卍”号，有的还会在房梁上画很多白粉点，表示人寿粮丰。

Similar to what the Han people do for the New Year, the compatriots in Tibet attach much importance to the Tibetan New Year. Most of them begin to make arrangements connected to the festival half a month in advance, including frying cakes and preparing boiled mutton, buttered tea, milk tea, wine made of highland barley and some other holiday food. Take the areas of Lhasa as example: before the supper on the twenty-ninth day of the twelfth month by the lunar Tibetan calendar, people there would scatter the dry powder on the clean central wall of the kitchen in an auspicious pattern and draw on the door the mark "卍", which symbolizes luck and eternality, with concrete powder. Sometimes, they would draw lots of dots with white powder on the beams of the house, implying longevity and bumper harvests.

除夕夜，家家户户都要吃团圆饭，吃一种名叫"古突"的面团土粑。这种土粑里往往还要故意包进去一些东西，有石子、辣椒、木炭、羊毛等。谁吃到了这些东西，就要当场吐出来，引起哄堂大笑。这些东西各有其象征意义，据说，吃到石子，预示此人在新的一年里心肠很硬；吃到木炭，预示此人心里黑；吃到辣椒，表示嘴如刀；吃到羊毛，说明心肠很软，如此等等，不一而足。

On Tibetan New Year's Eve, every family will eat Gutu, a kind of flour Tuba for the family reunion dinner. Usually, the dumpling Tubas are filled with some surprising objects like stones, chili, charcoal and wool. He who happens to have Tuba with these objects must spit them out in public, setting everybody present roaring with laughter. All these objects have their symbolic meanings. It is said that he who has Tuba with stones will be seen stone-hearted in the year to come; with charcoal, cruel-hearted; with chili, sharp-tongued; with wool, kind-hearted. Actually, similar cases are numerous.

按照藏族的风俗习惯，年夜饭每人都要吃九碗，每次不能吃完，把吃剩的食物倒在一个盆里，在吃完饭之后端着盆，打着火把，到各个房间去转悠，俗称“赶鬼”。

According to the Tibetan customs, at the dinner on that night, each family member should have nine bowls of food, and each bowl must contain some leftovers, which are to be put into a basin. After dinner, the family, with the illumination of a torch, hold the basin and stroll in every room, known as driving-away-ghosts.

除夕夜，家家房顶上都燃起象征吉祥的松脂，门窗上挂起“祥布”，桌柜上陈列各种点心。还有一种五谷斗，里边装着糌粑、炒麦粒、人参果等食品，上面插着青穗、鸡冠花，藏语叫做“竹素琪玛”；再是一个用彩色酥油花塑的羊头，藏语叫做“洛过”，也一起陈列在桌柜上。桌柜上方挂松赞干布、文成公主的画像，或是神像，以示虔诚。这些陈列，标志着过去一年的丰收，也是预祝新的一年会更好。

On New Year's Eve, the pine rosin, symbolizing good lucks, is lit on the roof of each house; pieces of “auspicious cloth” are hanging on the windows and doors; varieties of desserts are laid on the tables. There is also a kind of rectangular container, known as Zhusu Qima in Tibetan. It is fully loaded with Zanba, roasted wheat, ginseng fruits and the like, into which ears of highland barleys and cockscombs are planted. Besides, a sheep head molded in colorful butter

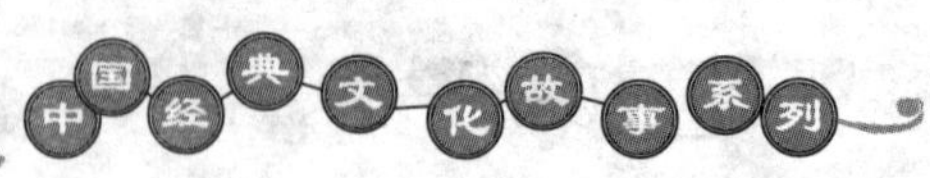

flowers, called Luoguo in Tibetan, is also laid on the table. The people also put the pictures of Songtsen Gampo and Princess Wencheng or statues of gods on the table to show their piety for them. This kind of exhibition marks the bumper harvests achieved in the past year and their best wishes for the coming year.

年初一凌晨，家庭主妇要到河旁井边背回一桶“吉祥水”，让全家起床洗漱，还要给牲畜饮用。全家坐定后，母亲端起“竹素琪玛”，向全家祝福，每人从“竹素琪玛”里抓一点糌粑，抛向空中，表示祭神，接着依次品尝少许，回祝母亲安乐康健。然后，大家在一起吃早饭，互敬青稞酒。孩子们则燃放鞭炮，表示庆贺。

On the early morning of the New Year's Day, housewives should carry home a bucket of auspicious water from the river for the other family members to wash their faces and for the domestic animals to drink. After the family members sit down, the mother carries "Zhusu Qima" and says prayers to them. They then take a little Zanba out of it one by one and scatter it in the air to represent their sacrifices to the gods. After that, they taste a little of it, show their best wishes for their mother's health and happiness, have breakfast together and then offer the wine made of highland barley to each other. By contrast, children celebrate this festival by setting off firecrackers.

年初一，藏族同胞一般不出门。从初二开始，亲朋好友间互相拜年，献哈达，主人捧着“竹素琪玛”迎客，拿出最好吃的食品款待客人，宾主歌舞联欢，往往会通宵达旦。节日里，人们相约到林卡游玩，各地演唱藏戏，跳锅庄舞和弦子舞，有的地方往往还要赛马、赛牦牛、角力、射箭、拔河，把节日的气氛营造得格外热烈，让人难以忘怀。

On the New Year's Day, the people usually stay at home. On the second day of the New Year, relatives and friends visit each other and present Hadas mutually. The host entertains the guests with the most delicious food from the Zhusu Qima. Afterwards, they often dance and sing all through the night. During the festival, people also go out to play in Linka together and they can enjoy the Tibetan plays and songs everywhere, among which the Guozhuang and Xuanzi dances are very popular. In some places, people celebrate the festival by holding activities like horse racing, yak racing, wrestling, archery and tug-of-war, which make the festive atmosphere especially warm and unforgettable.

十四、那达慕大会

14. The Nadamu Festival

那达慕大会，又称“那达慕”、“那雅尔”，是蒙古族的传统节日。那达慕，是“游戏”、“欢乐”的意思。时间一般在春夏之交，农历七八月间。这个季节里，草原上的五畜肥壮，正是挤马奶的时节。

The Nadamu Festival, also known as Nadamu or Laya’er, is a traditional festival observed by the Mongolian ethnic group. As a Mongolian term, Nadamu means “game” and “entertainment”. The festival is celebrated at the turn between spring and autumn, that is, between the seventh and the eighth lunar month, when the pastures there have such stout and strong domestic animals as oxen, dogs, sheep, pigs, and chickens. It is also the best season for the people to milk the mares.

一般认为那达慕起源于古代的“祭敖包”。“敖包”是以石块堆积而成的祭坛，祭祀对象称为“鄂博”，信仰喇嘛教的民族都有这种祭祀风俗。蒙古族祭敖包时，十分隆重，男女老少，携带哈达、整羊肉、奶酒和奶食，来到敖包处，献上哈达和供品，由喇嘛诵经祈祷，众人跪拜，祈求神灵保佑，镇住邪魔，降赐吉祥，

人畜平安，五谷丰登。然后往敖包上添加石块或以柳条修补，并悬挂新的五色绸布条和经幡。祭祀仪式结束以后，人们就在那里举行赛马、摔跤、射箭等各种游艺活动。这种风俗后来逐渐被固定下来，称为“那达慕大会”。

The festival is generally believed to derive from the ancient Aobao Sacrificial Ceremony, which is a custom among the people believing in Lamaism. “Aobao” is an altar piled up with stones and he who is offered sacrifices is called “Ebo”. The Mongolian Aobao Sacrificial Ceremony is quite ceremonious. During this ceremony, the people, male and female, young and old, come to the Aobao to offer their sacrifices like Hadas, the mutton of a whole sheep, milky wine, and milky food. While lamas are chanting the sutras and praying, the people kneel down, praying to be blessed by gods with good luck, safety of both people and animals, a golden harvest, and the suppression of the evil spirits. Then, people add stones to the Aobao or supplement it with twigs and hang new strips of five-coloured cloth and flags with lections. After the sacrificial ceremony, activities like horse-racing, wrestling, archery and the like are held there. Later on, this kind of customs is gradually fixed as the Nadamu Festival.

传说，汉代王昭君出塞，草原人民就曾经以这种盛大的活动迎接过她，可见由来已久。铭刻在石崖上的《成吉思汗石文》则说，当年成吉思汗为了庆祝胜利，在布哈苏齐海地方，也就是今天的新疆、甘肃边界，举行了一次盛大的那达慕大会。元明两代，射箭、赛马和摔跤三项比赛已经成为那达慕的固定形式。后来还增加了说书、歌舞、下棋等项目，如今则又有了电影放映、展览、贸易市场和各种文化经济交流活动，愈发丰富多彩起来。

The Nadamu Festival has a long history. It is believed that Nadamu entertainments were offered by the people living on the pastures in honor of Wang Zhaojun, who, by the Han Dynasty (206 BC — 220 AD) emperor's arrangement, came from China's inland to marry the Xiongnu Chieftain. According to the "Stone Inscriptions of Genghis Khan", inscribed on a cliff, Genghis Khan, the first emperor of the Yuan Dynasty (1271 AD — 1368 AD), held a very grand

Nadamu Festival in the area of Buhe Suqi Sea, now known as the border areas between Xinjiang and Gansu, to celebrate his success. The Nadamu Festival celebration had been organized regularly and officially in the forms of archery, horse-racing, and wrestling during the Yuan and Ming dynasties (1271 AD—1644 AD). Afterwards, other items like storytelling, singing and dancing, chess-playing and the like were included in the forms. Nowadays there are also movies, exhibitions, trading markets, and various activities of cultural exchanges, for which the festival activities become strikingly various and colourful.

赛马是最能表现蒙古族男子汉气概的项目。游牧民族，个个能骑善射。射手在颠簸的马背上射箭，更需要极高的技巧。骑马射箭的场面汹涌澎湃，激奋人心，自不待言。蒙古族的摔跤也闻名遐迩，摔跤不仅是力量的角逐，同时也是智慧和技巧的较量。无论胜败，人人的身心都得到了极大的欢愉。而当激烈的比赛之后，马头琴声又在草原上响起，人们纵情歌舞，通宵达旦，意犹未尽。这样的狂欢节日当然是令人难以忘怀的。

Horse-racing is the very item which can demonstrate the masculinity of the Mongolian men. As a nomadic race, every Mongolian man is talented in riding and shooting, whereas to shoot on the bumpy back of a horse requires the shooter's superb shooting skills. It is needless to say that the scenes of the horse-racing and archery are quite tempestuous and exciting. As far as wrestling is concerned, it is equally exciting, for it is not only the match of strength but also the match of wisdom and skills. Whoever fails or succeeds in the match can definitely achieve extreme pleasure both physically and mentally. After these fierce competitions, the pastures begin to be filled with the sweet lingering music of the Matouqin and the people are lost in singing and dancing all through the night, too joyful to be described. No doubt, such a revelous festival will remain a good memory forever in people's minds.

十五、古尔邦节

15. Id al-Qurban

古尔邦节是信仰伊斯兰教民族的节日，与开斋节、圣纪节并称为伊斯兰教三大节日。我国回、维吾尔、哈萨克、乌兹别克、塔吉克、塔塔尔、柯尔克孜、撒拉、东乡、保安等民族都要过这个节日。

Id al-Qurban is a festival celebrated by Islam. Id al-Qurban, Id al-Fitr and Mawlid al-Nabi comprise the three main Islamic festivals. The celebration is observed in different ethnic groups in China, such as the Hui, Uygur, Kazak, Uzbek, Tajik, Tatar, Kirgiz, Salar, Dongxiang and Bonan.

古尔邦节，又称宰牲节、献牲节、忠孝节、大会礼日、库尔班节、尔德节，在每年伊斯兰教历的十二月十日举行。伊斯兰教历纪元是从穆罕默德由麦加迁徙到麦地的那一年算起的，相当于公元622年。伊斯兰教历每年要比公历少十天或十一天，又没有闰年闰月，所以如按公历计算，就很难说出这个节日的固定时间了。

Id al-Qurban is also called Id al-Adha, Feast of the Sacrifice, Zhongxiao Festival, Salat al-’Id, Korban Festival or al-’Id al-Saghir, etc. in different ethnic groups. It falls on

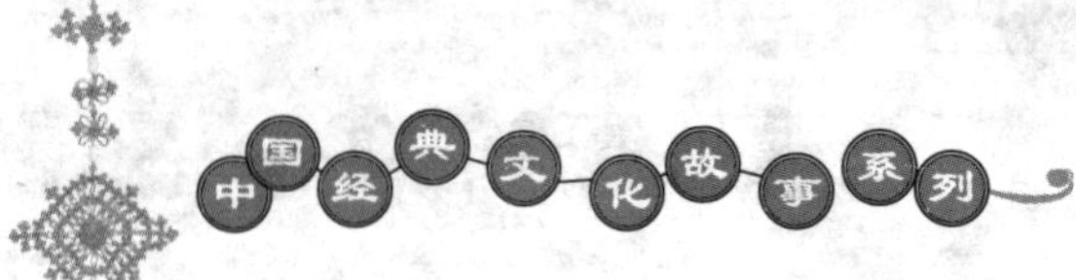
中国经典文化故事系列

the 10th day of the twelfth month of the Islamic calendar. The beginning of Islam calendar started from the year when Muhammad migrated from Mecca to Medina, approximately 622 A.D. We cannot set the festival by the Gregorian calendar, for the Islamic calendar has 10 or 11 days fewer than the Gregorian calendar, and it has no leap years or leap months.

古代阿拉伯传说，先知易卜拉欣受到安拉的启示，命他宰杀自己的儿子易司玛仪作为献祭，以考验他对安拉的虔诚。后来，安拉又派了个天使，牵一头羊赶到现场，命易卜拉欣以宰羊来代替献子。从此以后，古代阿拉伯人就有了每年宰牲献祭的风俗。伊斯兰教继承这一风俗，并规定这一天为宰牲节。随着伊斯兰教传入中国，这个节日也传了进来，成为信奉伊斯兰教的中国少数民族的传统节日。

An ancient Arabian legend goes like this: Prophet Ibrahim bowed to Allah’s command and prepared to sacrifice his son Isma’il. Later, an angel was sent to replace Ibrahim’s son with a sheep before he actually sacrificed his most beloved son. The custom of sacrificing an animal was thus passed down among the ancient Arabians. The Islam followed the custom and set the day as Id al-Adha. The festival was introduced to China when Islamism spread across China, and it is now a traditional festival celebrated by those ethnic groups in China who believe in Islamism.

为了献牲，他们在接羔时就已经在做准备了。产羔时，选定作为献牲的羔羊，要做上标记，从此不准打骂它，更不可出售和宰杀。节前，家家户户要打扫庭院，制作油香、馓子、烤馕、糕点等各种节日食品。

The preparation of sacrifice starts from the delivery of lambs. The lamb for sacrifice is chosen at its delivery and is made a mark. No one is allowed to beat it, curse it, sell it or kill it. Before the festival, all households should clean their yards, make various festival food like the Muslim flour-and-salt cake fried in sesame oil, deep-fried dough twist, roast crusty pancake, and cakes.

节日拂晓，人们起床后就要沐浴，燃香，穿上节日盛装，赶到清真寺去参加会礼。有的在一路上还要诵经赞主。穆斯林们齐集清真寺后，由阿訇或教长率领步入大殿，面向圣地麦加方向鞠躬叩拜，阿訇宣讲教义。最后，大家相互拜会。会礼之后，还要举行宰牲仪式，一般人家都要宰一只羊，有的还要宰牛或骆驼。宰牲的肉，通常会分成三份：一份自家人食用；一份送亲友邻居，招待客人；一份济贫施舍。

At daybreak, after getting up, everyone has a shower, lights incense, goes to the mosque for a gathering in his festival best. Some chant scriptures on the way there. After the Muslims gather in the mosque, the imam leads them to the main hall. They bow and kowtow in the direction of Mecca, the Holy Land. The imam preaches. Then the people begin to greet each other. The ceremony of sacrificing animals is held. A sheep is sacrificed by ordinary households, while a cow or a camel is offered by rich ones. The meat is divided into three shares, for themselves, for the neighbors and friends, and for the needy.

宰牲典礼结束以后，开始走亲访友，相互贺节，馈赠节日礼品。主人总会按照传统礼节，摆出丰盛的宴席，款待客人。

After the ceremony, people begin to pay visits to their friends and relatives with holiday greetings and gifts. According to the tradition, the hosts entertain the guests with a luxurious feast.

这一天的活动内容很多，不同的民族也会有所不同。有的还会在这一天游坟扫墓，诵经祈祷，缅怀先人。新疆维吾尔族要举行盛大的麦西来甫歌舞集会。牧区的哈萨克、柯尔克孜等民族则要举行叼羊、赛马、摔跤等活动。特别是他们那儿盛行的“姑娘追”，更是别具一格。青年男女各骑一匹马，骑马并行，向指定目标慢步行进。一路上，小伙子可以向姑娘尽情逗趣，倾吐爱情，姑娘不得生气。等到了指定地点，形势顿时逆转，小伙子必须策马迅速折回，姑娘则紧追不舍，并举鞭抽打对方，小伙子不可以抗拒。当然，这中间的情况往往会有微妙的变化，倘若姑娘真的看中了这个小伙子，她的皮鞭当然就不会真的打下去了。“姑娘追”常常成为青年男女谈恋爱的独特方式，浪漫而又别致，这在别的地方是很少能够见到的。

A lot of activities are held on this day, and they differ among different ethnic groups. Some pay tribute to their deceased ones at their tombs, chant scriptures and pray to memorize their ancestors. The Uygurs hold a grand party of Maixilaipu folk songs and dances. The Kazakstans and Khalkhases in pastureland have their special ways of celebrating the festival. There are activities like goat-tussle, horse-racing and wrestling. Another special and prevalent activity is “Girl-chasing”. A lad and a lass ride horses slowly toward the destination. On the way there, the lad tries his best to amuse the lass and express his love, while the lass is not allowed to get angry. Things are different on their way back. The lass chases the lad on horseback and beats him with her whip, while the lad is not allowed to resist. There can be subtle changes if the lass loves the lad. She would sway her whip symbolically for a couple of times over the lad’s head. “Girl-chasing” is a special way for the youngsters of these ethnic groups to express their love. Romantic as it is, it is not observed in other places.

十六、开斋节

16. Id al-Fitr
(The Fast-Breaking Festival)

开斋节是信仰伊斯兰教民族的又一个重大节日，又称“肉孜节”、“大开斋”、“大节”、“大年”、“大聚”、“大尔德”、“小尔德”等。

Another very important Islamic holiday is Id al-Fitr (the Fast-Breaking Festival), which is also referred to as the Rozah Festival, the Greater Feast, al-'id al-Kabir, Id al-Fitr, id al-Kabir or id al-Saghir etc.

伊斯兰教教法规定，每年伊斯兰教历九月是教徒斋戒的月份，大家都要斋戒一个月，称为“斋月”。斋月的最后一天，如果看见了新月的月牙，第二天，一般也就是伊斯兰教历的十月一日，就可以开斋了。这一天就是开斋节。如果那天晚上没见到新月，则还要继续斋戒，直到看见新月的月牙为止。一般说来，这种顺延不会超过三天。

According to the Islamic law, known as Shariah, the ninth month of the Islamic calendar is the month of fast or Ramadan. During the month, the Hui Muslims abstain from any food and conjugal relations. The Fast-Breaking Festival follows

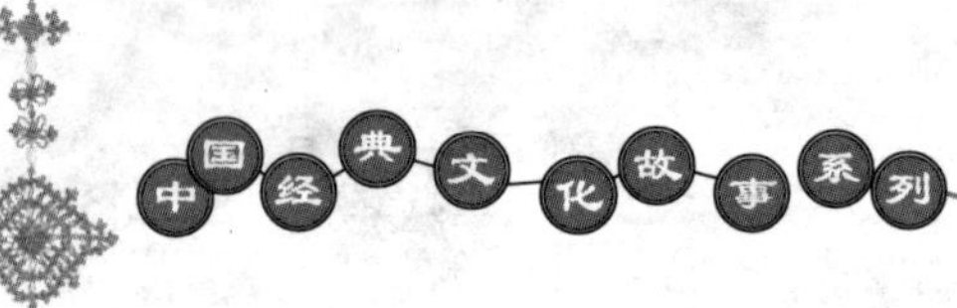
中国经典文化故事系列

the month of Ramadan, usually falling on the first day of Shawwal (the tenth month in the Islamic calendar). As with all months in the Islamic calendar, it begins with the sighting of the new moon. If the new moon is not sighted the Ramadan month continues on for one more day, and then the new month starts. Generally, the Fast-Breaking Festival will only be postponed by three days at most.

关于这个节日的来源，在伊斯兰教经典上就有记载。据说，伊斯兰教初创时，穆罕默德在斋月满了的时候进行沐浴，然后身穿洁净的服装，率领众多穆斯林，步行到郊外旷野举行会礼，并散发开斋捐，表示赎罪。以后，这种做法世代相传，沿袭成为节日风俗。

The origin of the Fast-Breaking Festival recorded in classical Islamic texts goes like this: in the early days of Muslim the Prophet Muhammad would put on clean clothes after a fresh bath at the end of Ramadan and lead Muslims to walk to open fields for the Eid prayer, then, in order to redeem his sin, he sent them gifts, known as Sadaqa al-Fitr (charity money). Later the practice was passed down from generation to generation and developed into a custom.

在开斋节前，每个家庭成员都要向穷人发放开斋捐，进行施舍。人们还要粉刷房屋，打扫院落，尤其要把清真寺装饰一新。

家家户户杀鸡宰羊，炸油香、馓子，准备节日食品。开斋节当天的清晨，成年男子必须沐浴净身，身着盛装，或手持经香，聚集清真寺或出荒郊举行会礼。会礼结束后，或由阿訇率领着，集体游坟扫墓；或是各家各户去扫墓，为逝者祈祷。随后分头到亲戚朋友家拜节，互赠礼品祝贺。节日的第二三天，年轻夫妇和未来女婿要到岳父母家拜节。有的人家还会选择在节日里举行婚礼。

Before the festival it is customary for every family member to pay Sadaqa al-Fitr to the poor or needy. People also paint or clean their houses and most importantly decorate the mosques. Every household slaughters goats and makes deep-fried dough twists and puffed fritters (pieces of fried bather, usually with sliced fruit in it). On the morning of the Fast-Breaking Festival after taking a fresh shower, female adults are dressed in their best clothes, sometimes carrying joss sticks in hand to attend a special Eid prayer that is performed in congregation at mosques or open fields. After the whole ceremony is over, Islam Ahung (the officiating priest of a mosque) leads the congregation to their ancestors' graveyard to mourn the deceased, while in some cases people may go there separately without Ahung. Then Muslims usually scatter to visit various family and friends, exchanging gifts with each other. During the following two or three days, young couples or the would-be husband will visit the wife's or the fiancée's parents. The young people usually choose to have their weddings during these days as well.

除此之外，还有许多群体性的节日活动。甘肃、青海一带，节日里往往要举行唱花儿、摔跤、掰手腕、拔腰、拧手指头等活动；在哈萨克、塔吉克、柯尔克孜等民族中间，则会举行叼羊、赛马、斗羊、射箭等活动。节日里的马也与平时不同，马身上扎满红色布标，系着各种花饰和野鸡毛，格外漂亮。

Besides, there are many other organized activities. For example, around Gansu and Qinghai provinces, people celebrate the festival by singing Hua'er (a form of folk song), wrestling, arm wrestling and thumb wrestling, etc. Among Kazakh, Tajik and Kirghiz people diaoyang (riders competing for a headless goat), horse racing, goat fighting, arrow shooting are popular. The horses are extraordinarily beautiful, decorated with red cloths, flowers and pheasant feathers.

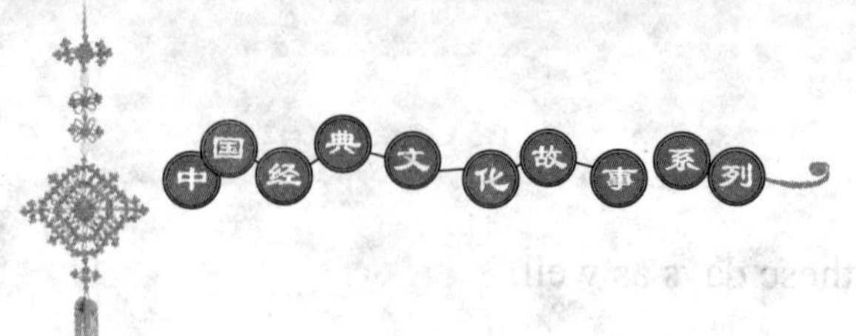

十七、圣纪节

17. Mawlid al-Nabi

圣纪节，又称“圣忌”，与古尔邦节、开斋节并称为伊斯兰教三大节日。伊斯兰教历十一年（公元632年）三月十二日，是穆罕默德的逝世日，也有的说是穆罕默德的诞生日，总之，信仰伊斯兰教的民族都把这一天称为“圣忌”，为缅怀穆罕默德的功德，举行隆重的纪念活动，世代相传，成为节日。

Mawlid al-Nabi, Id al-Qurban and Id al-Fitr are the three important Islamic festivals. The 12th of the third month of year 11 in the Muslim calendar (632 AD) was said either to be the day of Muhammad's death or his birth. It was taken as Mawlid by all the Islamic nationalities to honor his contributions in the form of ceremonious memorial events which were passed down from generation to generation and developed into a festival.

穆斯林都把“圣纪节”这一天的义务劳动当做行善做好事，大伙儿十分踊跃，有的自愿捐赠粮、油、肉和钱物。大家一齐动手，把清真寺布置得十分气派，四周张灯结彩，扎牌坊，挂彩旗。这一天，穆斯林都要沐浴，然后聚集在清真寺诵经、赞圣、礼拜。阿訇宣讲穆罕默德的生平轶事和功绩品德，教育后人不忘圣人教诲，做一个真正的穆斯林。这一天，穆斯林还要“讨白”，也就是忏悔的意思，表示痛改前非，求主饶恕。

The Muslims advocate that people should do good deeds voluntarily on that day, so everyone is active in donating cereals, oil, meat, money and other things generously, fixing the mosque up grandly with lanterns and colorful flags, and making memorial archways. They must take a shower that day and then gather together at the mosque to chant scriptures, sing praise of the saint and do religious services. Ahong preaches Muhammad's biography, values and qualities, and teaches the descendants not to forget the Saint's instructions and to be real Muslims. The Muslims also have the performance of repenting their sins and begging for forgiveness on that day.

仪式结束后，一般都要会餐。有的清真寺要炸油香、宰牛宰羊，设盛宴款待；也有的则将牛、羊肉分成若干份，凡参加纪念活动的，每户可以领到一份。各家各户，往往也要设宴待客，节日的气氛十分浓郁。

The ceremony is followed by a feast for which the Muslims do the frying and butcher cows and sheep, while in other mosques the beef and mutton are divided into certain portions and every family at the rite can get one share. Families also host a big dinner for guests at home and enjoy the lively festival atmosphere.

十八、尝新节

18. The Tasting-New-Rice Festival

尝新节，又称“吃新节”、“吃米节”。云贵高原上的土家、瑶、仡佬、苗、侗、彝、布依、纳西、普米、傈僳、拉祜、哈尼、景颇、阿昌、德昂、布朗、基诺等民族都要过这个节日。顾名思义，这是一种在丰收在望的时候或是收获之日的欢庆，人们在这时候举行祭祀，表示感恩。其实在一些汉族地区，历史上也曾有过“尝新”的风俗习惯，只是将其作为节日的意识可能已经不太强烈了。

The Tasting-New-Rice Festival is also called the Eating-New-Rice Festival or the Eating-Rice Festival. It is celebrated by many ethnic groups like the Tujia, Yao, Gelo, Miao, Dong, Yi, Buyei, Naxi, Pumi, Lisu, Lahu, Hani, Jingpo, Achang, De'ang, Bulang and Jino. Just as its name implies, this festival is an occasion to celebrate their harvest and to show people's gratitude to their ancestors through offering sacrifice to them. In fact, in some places where Han people live, there used to be a custom of tasting new rice though its festival sense was not so strong.

不同的民族，尝新节的时间安排、节日活动内容、祭祀方式都会有所不同，不过这中间所表达出来的对于劳动的尊重和对于

劳动果实的珍惜，则是相通的。

Although the date and festival activities vary with ethnic groups located in different areas, there is one thing in common about the festival—it expresses people's respect towards hard work and their homage for the fruit of labor.

德昂族在每年的农历六月里就要“尝新谷”了，而布朗族则总是安排在农历七月过节。他们要选择一个属蛇的日子，下地掐新谷。俗信以为，蛇吃东西不多，这就象征着谷物经吃。人们掐回新谷，边走边叫谷魂，一直叫进村寨，先将新谷送到佛寺及家神处供奉，祭拜之后，人们才开始煮新米饭吃。在大家开始吃饭之前，先要盛一碗新米饭慰劳牛和狗，然后众人才可以吃。

The De’ang ethnic people always taste new rice in the sixth lunar month, while the Bulang people choose to celebrate it in the seventh lunar month. They will choose a day of the snake according to the Twelve Earthly Branches, to pick the new rice in the field. The De’ang people believe that they will have rice to eat for a longer time since snakes eat little. When people are picking the new rice, they keep calling rice-soul back as they are walking to the village. The new rice will first be sent to the Buddhist temples and the family gods for sacrifice. After the rite, people begin to cook some newly-picked rice, but it is customary for them to feed their cows and dogs with the cooked rice before eating it themselves.

佤族的“新米节”，除了叫谷魂、祭祀神灵和祖先这些仪式之外，他们还会度过一个狂欢之夜。人们载歌载舞，尽情欢乐，用这种方式来庆贺丰收。

The Wa people, besides the rites of calling rice-soul back and sacrificing to their gods and ancestors, usually have a carnival night on this festival with songs and dances to celebrate their harvest.

苗族的吃新节又是一番气象。节前，家家户户都会邀请各自的亲戚朋友来家过节。主妇们到田间摘来新谷，舂成白米，蒸好新米饭，就邀请年老的客人，带着儿童来到田间，摆上新米饭和丰盛的菜肴，祭祀开田拓土的先人。下午，又会在广场上举行激动人心的斗牛比赛。此外，还有赛马、摔跤、拔河、斗雀等活动，异彩纷呈，让人目不暇接。当暮色降临的时分，姑娘和小伙子对唱情歌，跳起芦笙舞，节日的高潮也就终于到来了。

The Tasting-New-Rice Festival is also popular among the Miao ethnic group. Before the festival, every family will invite their relatives and friends to celebrate the day together. On the festival day, housewives will pick some new rice from the fields, husk and cook it. The well-cooked rice will be served together with delicious dishes in their fields to honor their ancestors who first opened up the wasteland for them. Only elderly guests, followed by children, are invited to such rites. In the afternoon, exciting bullfights will take place in the town squares. During the festival, there are many other interesting and attractive activities such as horse races, wrestling, tugs of war and sparrow-fighting. When the night falls, young men and women will pair off to sing round after round of love songs to each other and begin their Lusheng-flute dance, which

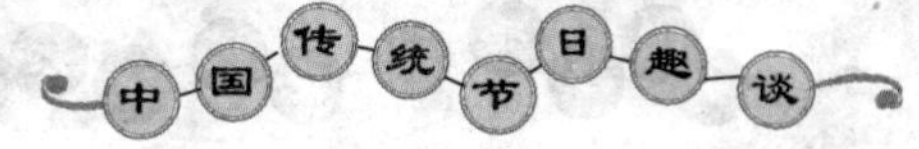

brings the day into its climax.

许多民族在尝新的时候都不会忘记狗，有的民族往往还一定要先让狗来吃新米饭，要等狗吃了之后，人们才开始吃。这种奇特的风俗又是怎么形成的呢？可能不同的学者也会作出不同的回答。不过非常有趣的是，在我国的许多民族中间，甚至也包括汉族在内，都曾经流传着一种关于狗偷谷种的神话，很值得我们注意。

It is interesting to notice that dogs play an important role in this festival. Many people will feed their dogs first with the cooked new rice before they taste it themselves. Although scholars may offer different explanations to this, it is an interesting fact that a myth about a dog stealing the seeds has long been told among many ethnic minorities, including the Hans.

这种神话都是说，早先的时候，人间是没有五谷的。后来，是动物帮了人类的大忙，从天上把谷种偷了下来。从此以后，人类才有了种植五谷粮食的历史。偷谷种的动物，有的民族说是鸟类，也有的民族说是老鼠，或是蚂蟥，但是更多的是说狗立下了汗马功劳。狗到天上去偷谷种，它先是把自己身上全打湿了，然后就地一滚，浑身都黏上了谷种。半路上要过一条天河，狗又翘起了自己的尾巴。结果呢，狗身上原先黏着的谷种全被水冲走了，尾巴上的谷种却被保留了下来。据说人类就是靠这些谷种繁殖五谷的，所以如今的五谷不可能从根到头都结籽，而只是顶上有一串，活像狗尾巴。人们还会说，你看，直到今天，狗一落水就会翘起尾巴，它还惦记着当年的事哩。

According to the myth, people did not have the five cereals in ancient times. Later, it was an animal who helped human beings out of hunger by stealing the seeds from Heaven and thus started the history of growing five cereals on the earth. As for the type of the animal who stole the seeds, some people say that it is a bird while some other people say that it is a mouse or a leech. But most people prefer to say that it is a dog who has made such a contribution. It is said that when the dog went up to Heaven to steal the seeds, it soaked itself all over and then rolled on the ground to get itself covered with seeds. On its way back to the earth, it crossed the Heaven River with its tail rolled high up. Consequently, all the seeds on its body were washed away by the water except those on its tail. It is said that it was these precious seeds that made it possible for people to grow food crops. That also explains why today's crops can produce grains only on the top, like the dog's tail. Some people still think that dogs can remember very clearly what happened in heaven because whenever they fall into water now, they will roll up their tails.

当然，神话并不就是信史。不过这里所传达出来的文化信息却又是那么珍贵。早期人类与动物之间亲密而又和谐相处的情景似乎又呈现在我们的眼前。重温这则神话，对我们理解“尝新节”的节日意蕴或许是有些帮助的。

After all, a legend is a legend. However, it does convey much valuable cultural connotations about the intimate relationships between animals and human beings, which can help understand the culture displayed in the Tasting-New-Rice Festival.

十九、泼水节

19. The Water-Splashing Festival

泼水节是云南西双版纳地区的傣、德昂、布朗、阿昌、佤族同胞共同的节日。傣语又称"楞贺尚罕"，是新年的意思。一般在每年公历 4 月 12 日左右举行，节期三至四天。阿昌族的泼水节则在农历五月二十三日。

The Water-Splashing Festival is a shared festival for many Chinese ethnic groups, such as the Dai, De'ang, Bulang, Achang, and Wa in Xishuangbanna, Yunnan Province of China. The Water-Splashing Festival is also called "Songkran", meaning the New Year in the Dai language. It usually occurs around April 12, and lasts for three or four days. But the Achang people celebrate it on the 23rd of the fifth lunar month.

泼水，主要是为了浴佛，作为一种宗教仪式，一般认为起源于印度。它起初是婆罗门教的一种古老仪式，后来又被佛教吸收，随着小乘佛教的传播，经由缅甸、泰国和老挝，传入我国的西双版纳地区，一般又称为"浴佛节"。发展到今日，人们在泼水浴佛之后，还要相互泼水，并形成狂欢场面，所以，就被称之为"泼水节"了。

To splash water, as a religious ritual, was originally to bathe the Buddha. Originated in India, to splash water was an ancient Brahmanist ritual. Later, it was observed by the Buddhist followers and spread, along with Hinayana, to Xishuangbanna, China, via Cambodia, Thailand and Laos, and it was also called the Buddha-Bathing Festival. As the festival evolves, people will sprinkle water at each other after they wash the dust off the Buddhist statues, which will quickly turn into a great rejoicing occasion. This is the so-called Water-Splashing Festival.

这时候正值傣历新年，所以这个节日又有辞旧迎新的意思在里面，犹如汉族的春节。头两天是辞旧，最后一天迎新。不同的民族，节日风俗活动又会有所不同，这里主要介绍傣族的泼水节。

As this festival falls on the Dai New Year, it gains the meaning of ringing out the Old Year and ringing in the New Year, similar to the Spring Festival of the Hans. People spend the first two days ringing out the Old Year and the third day ringing in the New Year. Different ethnic groups have different festival activities. The following is an introduction to the Water-Splashing Festival observed by the Dai people.

和汉族过年一样，傣族同胞在泼水节即将来临的时候就早已忙开了，杀猪宰鸡，酿酒，打年糕，做粑粑，制新衣，打扫卫生，里里外外都会焕然一新，形成浓浓的节日气氛。

Just as the Hans observe their Spring Festival, the Dai people usually begin their preparation for the Water-Splashing Festival long before it comes. Pigs and chickens are slaughtered, wines are brewed, the New Year cakes and the glutinous rice cakes are made, new clothes are sewed and the cleaning is done inside and outside every house, thus building up the strong festival atmosphere.

第一天清晨，青年男女成群结队上山，去采摘野花树枝，拿到佛寺献佛。他们还会在寺院中堆沙造塔，大伙儿围塔而坐，聆听念经。中午时分，人们把一尊佛像放置在院里，担来碧澄的清水浴佛，为佛像洗尘。

In the early morning on the first day, young men and

women swarm up the hills to pick wild flowers and branches to present to the Buddha in the temple. Once inside the temple, they will build sand castles and then sit around them listening to the scriptures. At noon, a Buddhist statue is placed in the yard and people begin to sprinkle water to bathe the Buddha with clear water.

宗教仪式之后，人们来到大街小巷，互相泼水，表示祝福。当地俗谚说："年年有个泼水节，看得起谁就泼谁。""水花放，傣家狂。"这时候不论是向别人泼水，还是被人泼了水，人人的脸上都洋溢着欢乐，以为只有这样才能吉祥如意。人们嬉戏追逐，全身湿透，却依旧乐此不疲。

After this religious rite, people come to the streets, sprinkling water onto each other as a way to express their best wishes. As the local proverb says, "on the Water-Splashing Festival every year, please sprinkle water onto those you think highly of," and "the more water are splashed, the more prosperous the Dai people will be." On this occasion, both the person who sprinkles water and the person who is sprinkled are beaming with pleasure, taking it as a way of obtaining good luck and happiness. Running and laughing, all the participants are soaked to the skin and intoxicated with pleasure and joy.

"赶摆"和"丢包"，也是泼水节风俗的亮点。"赶摆"是野外联欢活动。"丢包"则是未婚青年男女之间的一种游戏。男女青年分成两个阵营，相互丢花包。倘若小伙子接不住姑娘丢过来的花包，要在姑娘的孔雀髻上插一朵鲜花。倘若姑娘接不住小伙子丢过来的花包，也要在小伙子胸前插花。久而久之，其中有一对男女相互之间产生了好感，有了默契，飞舞着的花包便仿佛长上了眼睛，每次都能顺利到达对方的手中了。这是傣族青年男女谈情说爱的独特方式，浪漫而又温馨，令人难忘。

"Ganbai (visiting the local fair)" and "throwing floral bags" are also the highlights of the Water-Splashing Festival. "Ganbai" is a kind of happy get-together held in the open air while "throwing floral bags" is a game played between unmarried young men and women. The young people are divided into two camps, one of young men and the other of young women, throwing floral bags to each other. If a young man cannot catch the bag from a girl, he has to plug a flower on her coiled peacock bun. If a girl fails to catch the bag from a boy, she has to put a flower on his chest. With the lapse of time, a favorable impression and a tacit mutual understanding will develop between some boys and some girls. Then the bag tossing to and fro between them will always land in each other's hands, as if it had eyes. This is the unique Dai style of expressing love by young people, romantic and unforgettable.

节日里，澜沧江上还要举行激动人心的划龙船比赛。夜晚则燃放自己制作的烟火，青年人围着篝火尽情欢乐，演唱民歌，跳起孔雀舞、白象舞，通宵达旦，欢度节日。

During the festival, exciting dragon boat races will be held on the Lancang River. The festival nights will witness the beautiful fireworks made by the young people, who make merry to their hearts' content throughout the night until dawn, singing folk songs and doing the Peacock Dances as well as the Elephant Dances.

关于泼水节的由来，傣族有着一则动人的传说。说是很早以前，当地有个凶恶残暴的魔王，四处抢掠，无恶不作。他已经抢了十一个妻子还嫌不够，又去抢来了第十二个。妻子们对他恨之入骨，却没有办法可以害死他。

The Water-Splashing Festival originated from a sentimental legendary story. Long long ago, there lived a ferocious devil near where the Dai people lived. The devil did all kinds of evils to the residents. Although he had forced eleven girls to be his wives, he showed no sign of stopping and grabbed another girl as his twelfth woman. All his wives hated him to the marrow of their bones. Yet, no one could find ways to kill him.

新抢来的美女很有心计，她故意讨得魔王的欢心，终于从魔王嘴里探听到他的致命弱点，等他睡熟的时候，拔下他的一根头发，往他脖子上一勒，果然就把魔王的头勒了下来。

The new bride was a very intelligent young woman. She deliberately managed to win the devil's favor and to find out his mortal spot. When the devil was fast asleep, she pulled a hair from his head, twined it around his neck, and then, the devil's head was off his neck!

魔王死后，大家都兴高采烈。不过魔王的头仍然有魔力，十二个妻子先是想用火来烧，谁知火却越烧越大；她们把头埋在地下，地面上却发出极其难闻的臭味；她们把头抛到河里，河水居然会沸腾起来。到后来，十二个妻子只好轮流把魔王的头抱在怀里，她们每天换一次，轮流用水来冲洗。傣族民众为了感谢这十二个女子为民除害，为了表示对她们的敬意，就在这一天给她们泼水，久而久之，形成了节日风俗。

All the girls were wild with joy at the death of the devil. But as magic power still remained inside the devil's head, the twelve girls found it hard to subdue it. They tried to burn it with fire, only to find that the fire grew to an uncontrollable scale; they buried the head in the ground, but then stinking odor came out of the ground; they threw the head into a river, but then the water became boiling hot. At the last resort, the twelve girls had to take turns to hold the devil's head in their arms and to wash it with water, one girl each day. To their gratitude and respect for the twelve girls' contribution, the Dai people splash water on them on this day, which, with the passage of time, has gradually evolved into part of the local custom.

传说表达了傣族同胞对幸福生活的追求和对苦难深重的历史的一种追忆，可能有所附会，却也令人珍惜。总之，水是生命之源，互相泼水，表达了人们对于圣洁、美好的追求，这样一种象征意义，别的民族也都是能够理解的。

The legend, though a little farfetched, expresses the Dai people's aspiration for a happy life and their recollection of the miserable past. Anyhow, sprinkling water, the source of life, onto each other, conveys people's pursuit for the holly and good aspect of life, the symbolic feature of which is understandable to other nationalities.

二十、火把节

20. The Firebrand Festival

火把节是我国云南、四川、贵州、广西等地的彝、白、佤、哈尼、布朗、纳西、普米、傈僳、拉祜、基诺、仫佬、仡佬等民族的共同节日。火把节的时间，较多的民族都是安排在农历六月二十四五日开始，连续过三至七天；也有的民族安排在六月初六开始。

The Firebrand Festival is celebrated by such ethnic groups as the Yi, Bai, Wa, Hani, Bulang, Naxi, Pumi, Lisu, Lahu, Jino, Mulao and Gelao in Yun'nan, Sichuan, Guizhou and Guangxi of China. It is usually held on the 24th or 25th of the sixth lunar month and lasts for three to seven days, while some minorities start the celebration from 6th of the sixth lunar month.

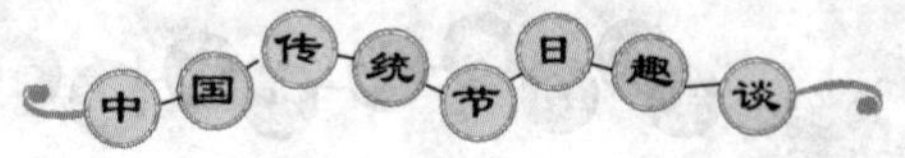

火把节的主要特征是点燃火把。节日里，家家户户都要在门前竖立起一个火把，或是燃烧一个火堆。村寨的公共场所则会竖起特大的火柱，火势冲天，光焰照人。人们还要手举火把到处游行，于是便形成了火的海洋，煞是壮观。一般认为，这里保存着“火崇拜”的某种历史记忆，是远古时代祭火仪式的流变。

The outstanding feature of the Firebrand Festival is to ignite the firebrand. During the festival, a firebrand is erected or a bonfire is enkindled in front of each house. Gigantic firebrands are placed in public places of the village, which send flames up to the sky and the sparkles illuminate people's excited faces. People hold a parade, a firebrand in hand, and thus an impressive magnificent sea of flames comes into sight. It is generally believed to be the preservation of the historical memory of "fire-worshipping", the evolution of fire-worshipping ceremonies from ancient times.

关于火把节的由来，不同的民族会有不同的解释，于是便有了许多动人的传说，虽然说法不同，莫衷一是，却都可以看做是各族民众对于历史的某种理解。

Different minorities have different interpretations of the origin of the Firebrand Festival; therefore many touching legends are recalled. Though none of these is considered to be the authoritative one, they stand for the different minorities' comprehension of history.

白族有这样一个动人的传说。说是一千多年前，洱海边上有六个部落，称为六诏。其中南诏势力最大，南诏王为了吞并其他五诏，就想出一条恶毒的计谋，造起一座松明楼，借口要举行六诏祭祖大典，邀请五诏王在六月二十四日都要来参加。邓赕诏王的妻子慈善夫人，又美丽又聪明，怀疑南诏王有阴谋，竭力劝阻丈夫，不要去参加。邓赕诏王很是为难，慑于南诏的势力，不得不去。临走时，慈善夫人找出一只铁手镯，套在丈夫手臂上。

The Bai minority has a moving tale from thousand years ago when six tribes called Six Zhaos dwelled by the Er Sea. The king of the most powerful tribe, the South Zhao, worked out a vice scheme to annex the other five Zhaos. He had a building named Songming established and invited the other five kings to come on the 24th of the sixth lunar month for the grand memorial ceremony in honor of ancestors. King Deng Dan's wife Ci Shan, who was beautiful and intelligent, thought that it was a trick and tried to stop her husband from going. Though in a dilemma, submitted to the power of the South Zhao, King Deng Dan had no choice but to go. Before his leaving, Ci Shan got out a bracelet and put it around his arm.

果然，六月二十四日这天，在祭祖大典之后，南诏王在松明楼宴请五诏王，把他们灌醉后，放一把火，五诏王全都葬身在火海之中。慈善夫人和其他各诏的亲属闻讯赶到现场，那里早已成为一片焦炭，死者面目全非，根本无法辨认。慈善夫人凭着铁镯才认出了丈夫的尸体。

Just as expected, on the 24th of the sixth lunar month, after the memorial ceremony, the king of the South Zhao gave a banquet to the five kings, got them drunk and set fire to kill them. On hearing the news, Ci Shan, together with the relatives of the other four Zhaos, hurried to the spot where everything had been scorched and the dead were burnt beyond recognition. Only by the bracelet, did Ci Shan identify her husband's body.

这时候，南诏王又想霸占慈善夫人。慈善夫人说要先将丈夫遗体运回本诏，妥为安葬，然后才可商议。南诏王无奈，只好答应。慈善夫人为丈夫办完丧事之后，就加紧训练士兵，加固城池，要与南诏王决一死战。后来，南诏王派兵马攻打邓赕诏，围城三个月，城里的粮食吃光了。慈善夫人把自己绑在椅子上活活饿死。临死时，她悲壮地对别人说："我要到上帝那儿去，为我丈夫申冤！"也有人说，慈善夫人是跳到洱海里自杀的。

Then the king of the South Zhao intended to take over Ci Shan by force. Ci Shan said that she wouldn't think of marrying him unless her husband's body be transferred back to her state first. The king of the South Zhao had to make a concession. After her husband's funeral, Ci Shan made great efforts to train her soldiers and strengthen the defense work for a life-and-death battle against the king of the South Zhao.

Subsequently, the army from the South Zhao attacked Deng Dan's Zhao; after three months' siege, Deng Dan's tribe ran out of food. Ci Shan had herself tied up to a chair and starved to death. Before her death, she said in a heroically tragic tone that she would go to pay homage to the god and ask him to redress the injustice done to her husband. There is still another version that Ci Shan jumped into the Er Sea and drowned herself.

当地的百姓为了纪念慈善夫人，每年六月二十四日这天都要高举火把来吊唁。

In memory of Ci Shan, the local people started the convention of the Firebrand Festival on the 24th of the sixth lunar month.

彝族有好几个支系，每个支系对于火把节的说法都不同。这里就先说说其中一个支系撒尼人的传说吧。

The Yi minority has several branches, each of which has its own version concerning the Firebrand Festival. Here is one of the Sani's.

撒尼人说，很早很早以前，天王觉得撒尼人的日子过得太好了，他就派大力神下凡，要毁掉大伙儿种的庄稼，让撒尼人再回到穿树叶、吃野果的年代。撒尼人跟大力神讲理，大力神当场斗败了几头牛，得意洋洋地说，你们看，我的力气大着呢。谁能摔倒我，我就转回天上，不管你们的事了。这时候，撒尼英雄朵阿惹恣站了出来，和大力神摔了三天三夜，最后终于把他赶走。这时候，天王还是不甘心，又撒下一把香炉灰，变成各种害虫，来嚼食庄稼。聪明的撒尼人就找来松树枝，点起一束束火把，去烧那些害虫，终于把害虫全烧死了。后来，人们把朵阿惹恣斗败大力神的那一天定为火把节，人人穿上节日的盛装，杀牛宰羊庆祝，还要举行斗牛、摔跤、打火把的活动。

As the legend goes, long long ago, the god of heaven thought that the Sani people did not deserve a good life and therefore he sent the god of strength to the earth to destroy the corn in order that the people would return to the life of being dressed in tree leaves and eating wild fruits. The Sani people tried to reason with the god, who, after defeating a few fierce bulls on the spot, said gloatingly that he would go back to Heaven and forgot his task if only anyone could beat him in a wrestling competition. Duo A're, the hero of the Sani people, rose to the challenge and after three days' wrestling the god was driven off. But the god of heaven was still unwilling to give up. From an incense burner, he cast ashes down to the earth, which turned into pests to chew off corns. The clever Sani people got pine branches to make firebrands and enkindled them to burn those pests. Eventually the pests were all burnt dead. Then the day on which Duo A're defeated the god of strength was regarded as the Firebrand Festival. In splendid attire, people slaughtered cows and sheep to celebrate the festival. Activities such as bullfighting, wrestling and firebrand-holding were also performed to add to the festive atmosphere.

拉祜族的火把节传说，说是当年山上有两个人，一个恶人，专门吃人眼睛。一个善人，见恶人要吃人眼睛，就去劝他别吃，又说自己可以拣田螺来给他吃。后来，恶人就专吃善人给他的田螺。不过田螺总有一天要吃完的，怎么办？善人就去买来一头山羊，给山羊安了一对蜂蜡做的角，晚上，点燃了山羊的角，让它上山去找恶人，准备送给恶人吃的。谁知道恶人弄错了，以为是山下的人抬着火药枪来找他报仇。他吓坏了，就到处逃，最后找了个岩洞躲了进去。山羊找不到恶人，也在山上乱跑，恶人又不敢出来，后来就死在岩洞里。从此以后，拉祜族同胞就要在这一天夜里举着火把上山，成为一个节日。

The Lahu minority's legend is about two people in the mountain, one vice person who ate only human eyes, and one good person who persuaded the vice one to give up the evil practice by saying that he would collect field snails for him to eat instead. Then the vice person began to eat only the field snails offered by the good person. But field snails were not inexhaustible. To solve the problem, the good person bought a goat, on whose head he put a set of horns made of honey wax. One night, he enkindled the horns and sent the goat up the mountain for the vice person to eat. But the vice person mistook it for people down the mountain coming up with

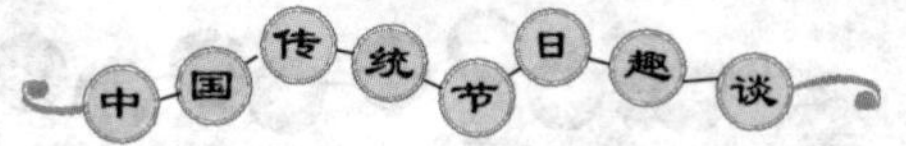

firearms for revenge. Astonished, he fled like a rat and finally hid himself in a cave. Having failed to find the vice person, the goat started to run wildly. Fearing to come out of the cave, the vice person was starved to death at last. Since then, the Lahu people began the celebration by going up the mountain with firebrands in their hands on the same night every year.

纳西族的火把节传说则又是一种说法。他们说，天神觉得纳西人的日子过得太好了，就派一个天神下凡，要放火烧人间。那个天将有些不忍心，就装扮成一个老公公到村寨去察访。半路上，他看见一个人，背着个大孩子，手里却牵着个小孩子。天将觉得奇怪，就问他为什么要这样做？那人说，大孩子是哥哥的儿子，小孩子是我的儿子。哥嫂都去世了，就剩下这个独苗苗，我应该格外疼爱他才是。这一说，天将也感动了，就悄悄地跟他说，六月二十五日，天神要到人间放火。你事先在门口竖个火把，就能免遭这场灾难啦。那人一听，大吃一惊，回到村寨，逢人就说，一传十，十传百，家家户户的门口都在这一天竖起了火把。天将一看，知道是那人走漏了消息，索性将错就错，对天神说，人间早已烧成一片火海啦。天神一看，果真如此，也就不再追究。从此以后，这里的人们就相沿成习，每到这一天都要点燃火把。大伙儿在火光里载歌载舞，祝愿人间大地更加繁荣昌盛。

The Naxi minority has a different version of the origin of the Firebrand Festival. It is said that the god of heaven thought the Naxi people were living a life they did not deserve, so he sent a minor god to set fire to the earth. The minor god had a

heart of sympathy and he dressed himself like an old man to make firsthand observations in the Naxi village. On the way, he came across a man carrying a big child on his back but dragging a small child with his hand. Out of curiosity, the minor god asked him why. The man answered that the big child belonged to his elder brother while the small child was his own, and that since his elder brother and sister-in-law had both passed away, he should lavish extra care and affection on this only child. Deeply moved, the minor god whispered to the man that on the 25th of the sixth lunar month the god of heaven would come to set fire to the earth, and that, to escape from the calamity, he should set up a firebrand in front of his house in advance. The man was taken aback and when he returned to the village, he revealed the secret to anyone he met. As a result, a firebrand was erected in front of each house on the 25th of the sixth lunar month. On the sight of this, the minor god knew it was the man who disclosed the secret; so he made the best of the mistake and reported to the god of heaven that the earth had become a sea of flames. Having taken a look at the earth, the god of heaven was convinced and did not make further investigation. Since then, it became a custom for the local people to ignite firebrands on the same night every year. Singing and dancing, they wished for a more thriving and prosperous earthly paradise.

二十一、丰年祭

21. The Harvest Festival

丰年祭，是台湾高山族同胞的盛大节日，相当于汉族人过年。时间一般是每年农历八月，人们通过祭祀祖灵，祈求来年丰收，人畜兴旺，故称“丰年祭”。节期一般要延续六至十天。

The Harvest Festival is celebrated by the Gaoshan people in Taiwan and is the most important one, equivalent to the Spring Festival of the Han people. It is held in the harvest season, usually in the eighth lunar month and lasts for six to ten days. As its name implies, people in the festival would offer sacrifices to their ancestors praying for a plentiful harvest and a growing family in the new year.

高山族的节日活动通常以“社”为单位。节前，社头通知各户，于是大家备办食品。除夕夜，妇女们聚集广场跳舞，男子则上山打猎，并在山上过夜。如今打猎之后可以回来，不过一般也都要在牛棚的阁楼上过夜。

Each village holds its own harvest festival. After the village head announces the start of the festival, families will prepare the food. Women gather on the village plaza to dance, while men go hunting in the mountains, where they stay for the night. Though they can come back home after hunting nowadays, they will still have to spend the night in the attic of their cowsheds.

节日里，要表演“钻木取火”。虽然如今他们早已用上了火柴和打火机，但是约定俗成，在这一天却要回到祖先的年代里去，体验古老的取火方式。第一次钻木取火，点燃兰芭子草，然后让它自燃自灭，过半小时，再一次钻木取火，用来煮糯米饭，蒸糕做菜。

During the festival it is customary for people to give a performance of making fire by rubbing instead of using matches or lighters, in order to experience what their ancestors did in ancient times. Fire is first made to light a plant called *lanbazi*, which is then left to go out by itself. Half an hour later, fire is made again to cook glutinous rice, cakes and other dishes.

然后，人们开始祭祀祖灵，唱起歌颂祖先的祭歌，妇女们在祖灵前跳“杵乐舞”，男子们则携带弓箭、刀枪，表演打猎过程。他们用这种方式祈求祖灵保佑，在新的一年里多打粮食，多获猎物。

Then comes the sacrificial ceremony, during which chants, pestle dances by women and hunting by men are performed to their ancestors as a prayer for blessings and a plentiful harvest in the next year.

“杵乐舞”是一种十分独特的民族舞蹈。杵，就是舂米时用的长木棒。长短粗细不同的杵撞击在石板上，就会发出高低不同的音响。一群妇女手执长杵，环绕在石臼四周，不断捣击石臼或是地面，由于不同的节奏，便形成了强烈的音响效果。虽然没有别的乐器伴奏，仅仅是靠长杵来撞击发声，却给人以强烈的震撼，让人们又回到了祖先生活的那个年代。杵乐舞还常常会伴以优美动听的杵歌，载歌载舞，令人难忘。

The pestle dance is a characteristic folk dance. The pestle is a long stick used to grind the rice. Different pitches are produced by striking pestles of different sizes on the stone. A group of women stand around a mortar and pound the mortar or the hard ground with long pestles, producing a strong sound effect with various rhythms. Though unaccompanied, the sound itself is extremely exciting, reminding us of the ancient times. Sometimes the dance will be performed together with

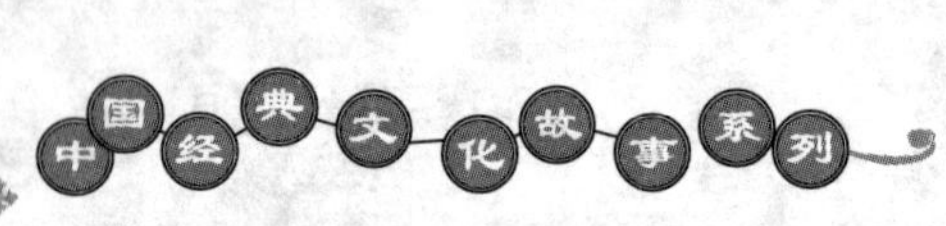

pleasant songs. Both the dancing and the singing are equally impressive.

节日的第二天，妇女们祭祖，男子则要到西边的山上去打猎，然后抬着猎物到主管历法的人家里，举行箭射兽头的活动，然后由部落首领将兽肉分给大家。

On the second day of the festival, while women continue with the sacrificial offerings, men will go hunting in the western mountains. When they come back with preys, they will go to the spiritual officiant's home for beast-head shooting activities, and after that, the tribal head will distribute the meat among people.

第三天晚上，要举行篝火舞会，称为“司马拉”。人们围绕篝火翩翩起舞，放声高唱“聚饮歌”。青年男女则趁此机会互诉爱情。

On the third evening a bonfire party is held, an occasion when people dance in a circle around the fire and sing "get-together songs". Boys and girls will have a chance to express their affections to each other.

一般在八月十五日还要举行“背篓会”，月亮初升时开始，日出前才结束。少男少女们在老年妇女的主持组织下，一起来到槟榔林，采摘槟榔，谈情说爱，情绪热烈欢快，别具一格。

There is usually a "back-basket party" on the night of the fifteenth day of the eighth lunar month at moonrise, often extending until daybreak. Organized by old women, young boys and girls gather on the areca farm to pick areca and it is concerned with love and romance. Everyone is happy and joyful on this special occasion.

最后一天，男人们还要一起到日月潭捕鱼，拿回来分给大家，象征着收获有鱼（余），丰年祭终于在欢声笑语中结束。

On the last day, men go to the Sun-Moon Lake for fishing together and then share the fish with others, suggesting that they have an abundant harvest. By then the Harvest Festival has come to an end with great cheers and laughter.